The Apostle Paul

An Introduction to His Writings and Teaching

Marion L. Soards

PAULIST PRESS
New York/Mahw

Library of Congress Cataloging-in-Publication Data

Soards, Marion L., 1952-
    The Apostle Paul.

        Includes bibliographies and index.
        1. Paul, the Apostle, Saint. 2. Christian
saints—Turkey—Tarsus—Biography.   3. Tarsus
(Turkey)—Biography.   4. Bible. N.T. Epistles
of Paul—Criticism, interpretation, etc.
5. Bible. N.T. Epistles of Paul—Theology. I. Title.
BS2506.S59   1986   225.9′24 [B]   86-25463
ISBN 0-8091-2864-0 (pbk.)

Published by Paulist Press
997 Macarthur Boulevard
Mahwah, New Jersey 07430

Printed and bound in the United States of America

Contents

Pauline Theology: An Overview of Paul's Thought

for Martha and David

Preface

"Why another book on Paul?" may be the justifiable reaction of those finding *this* book on a bookstore or library shelf. Even a cursory survey shows there is already a spate of volumes on Paul available to those interested in learning more about the Apostle to the Gentiles. To paraphrase Qoheleth (loosely), "Of the writing of books *on Paul* there is no end" (Eccl 12:12).

So, why this book on Paul? Perusal of the platoon of Paul books shows that the works fall into three categories: scholarly monographs, collected essays, and books for a mythical general audience. Whatever the character of these contributions, they usually seek to serve one of three aims: to produce a *life* of Paul, to examine *a letter or the letters* of Paul, or to summarize Paul's *theology* in general or on some particular point. Rarely, a book pursues two goals, as does Günther Bornkamm's *Paul*, which treats both Paul's life and his theology. Perhaps Bornkamm's ambitious format as much as the quality of his scholarship has made his book the standard text for Paul courses for more than a decade. The book continues to be the standard introductory text to Paul despite being the product of an interpretative approach that the majority of contemporary critical scholars considers to be less-than-adequate. And so, teachers and students of Paul cry out for a new text.

The Apostle Paul is, on the one hand, daring, and, on the other, reckless in seeking to speak to all three areas of Pauline studies—life, letters, and theology. With the overload of Paul books, nothing short of this approach seems suitable for a new book on Paul. Paul's life, letters, and theology must be treated together, since to do otherwise is to risk distorting one or more of the areas of Pauline studies. Moreover, one encountering Paul *needs* information regarding all three

1

areas, and no such book exists—especially one that understands Paul from the apocalyptic perspective which characterizes this study.

Thus, even though there are perils in this Pauline project, the task is undertaken. The format and much of the contents of this book developed and were refined in teaching Paul to both advanced undergraduate students and primary level (on Paul) seminarians. To those partners in Pauline studies at Louisiana State University and Union Theological Seminary, New York, I owe thanks for the motivation to produce this work designed to introduce the mission and message of one whose labors and thinking form an essential part of the foundation of all subsequent Christianity.

The work of many scholars influenced much of the understanding of Paul set forth in this book. Among those to whom I am particularly beholden are J. Christiaan Beker, Dieter Georgi, Ernst Käsemann, Leander E. Keck, Helmut Koester, Wayne A. Meeks, and, above all, J. Louis Martyn. Experts in biblical studies will recognize my indebtedness to these and many others, but in consideration of the nonprofessional readers, I have not freighted this work with scholarly footnotes; yet those readers who desire to plunge deeper into Pauline studies will find pointers in the bibliographies included throughout the book.

BIBLIOGRAPHY

There are many excellent books available to guide and assist the study of Paul. Among the best are

J. C. Beker, *Paul the Apostle* (2d ed.; Philadelphia: Fortress, 1984).

G. Bornkamm, *Paul* (New York: Harper & Row, 1971).

F. F. Bruce, *Paul: Apostle of the Heart Set Free* (Exeter: Paternoster, 1977).

R. Bultmann, *Theology of the New Testament,* two volumes in one (New York: Scribner's Sons, 1951/1955).

E. Käsemann, *Perspectives on Paul* (Philadelphia: Fortress, 1971).

L. E. Keck, *Paul and His Letters* (Philadelphia: Fortress, 1979).

W. G. Kümmel, *Introduction to the New Testament* (17th ed.; Nashville: Abingdon, 1975).

W. A. Meeks, ed., *The Writings of St. Paul* (Norton Critical Edition; New York: Norton, 1972).

D. Patte, *Paul's Faith and the Power of the Gospel* (Philadelphia: Fortress, 1983).

C. J. Roetzel, *The Letters of Paul* (2d. ed; Atlanta: Knox, 1985).

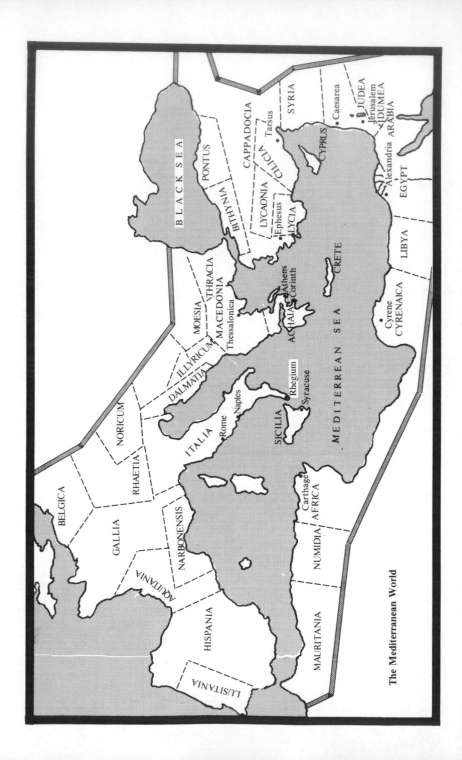

The Mediterranean World

Paul the Man:
Life and Work

Reconstructing Paul's Life

The best place to start thinking about the apostle Paul is with the man himself. What can be known of him and how can it be known? The New Testament and other early Christian literature seem to provide a wealth of sources for reconstructing the life of Paul. Over one-half of the Book of Acts is a long, important account of Paul's career from the time he was a persecutor of the church through his imprisonment in Rome toward the end of his life. Thirteen letters in the New Testament bear Paul's name as their author. Outside the canon of the New Testament many volumes of early Christian literature present themselves as "other" letters by Paul or offer further accounts of his "acts."

Problems in the Use of the Sources

When one turns to the early Christian literature in order to ascertain the life of Paul, one immediately encounters three serious problems. First, extensive as the sources are, they provide *insufficient data* for writing a "life" of Paul. For example, little, if anything, is known about Paul's birth, childhood, and early manhood; indeed, we do not even know with absolute certainty when, where, and how Paul died. Much remains shrouded in mystery, for the sources are simply inadequate for producing a Pauline biography.

Second, one must establish the *authenticity* of the sources. For example, no contemporary scholar judges that Paul wrote any of the number of extrabiblical letters that are attributed to him, correspondences like "the Epistles of Paul and Seneca," "Paul's Letter to the Laodiceans," and "3 Corinthians." Clearly these were produced by others in the name of Paul. Moreover, because of matters of history, vocabulary, style, and theology, many scholars (frequently the majority) judge that as many as six of the thirteen letters in the New Testament attributed to Paul were written by his colleagues and students, not the apostle (see the Appendix, Pauline Pseudepigrapha and Pseudepigraphy). These are 2 Thessalonians, Ephesians, Colossians, 1 and 2 Timothy, and Titus. Only seven letters are judged undisputedly to be authentic. For now, it is sufficient for one to recognize that all of the New Testament letters attributed to Paul are not considered to be of equal value for reconstructing the life of the apostle. This position in no way lessens the importance of the six debated letters. Regardless of decisions related to their authorship, these letters are part of the canonical New Testament—indeed part of the canonical Pauline corpus—and merit consideration as such. Thorough attention will be given to the authorship of those letters which scholars debate as we examine the Pauline literature below.

Third, it is sometimes *impossible through harmonization to reconcile statements* made in even the most reliable sources. For example, Acts 9 recounts that when Paul was struck down on the road to Damascus, he was "immediately" active there (in Damascus) preaching in the synagogues that Jesus was the Son of God. After "many days," Acts says, he went to Jerusalem in an effort to *join* the disciples; but they were afraid of him, because they doubted his sincerity, and so they avoided him. Then one learns from Acts that Barnabas took Paul to the apostles who accepted him. The result was that Paul preached, going in and out among the Jerusalem Christians and even down to Caesarea, so that "the church throughout all Judea and Galilee and Samaria had peace and was built up" (Acts 9:31).

In contrast, Gal 1:11–24 (especially verses 15–24) is a statement by Paul declaring his independence as an apostle. He avers here that the gospel he preached did not come from any human; instead it came through a revelation by God of the risen Jesus Christ. Paul claims he was ordained by God, that he did not confer with "flesh and blood," i.e., any human agent. He insists that when he was called by God he did not go up to Jerusalem to the apostles for their approval but went to Arabia and later returned to Damascus. He says that after three years he visited Cephas (Simon Peter) in Jerusalem for fifteen days; but he declares that he saw "none of the other apostles except James the Lord's brother" (Gal 1:19). Indeed, Paul claims that he departed after this visit "still not known by sight to the churches of Judea" (Gal 1:22).

The usual harmonization of these passages has Paul, Peter, and James skipping off arm-in-arm down "the Way" like the Tinman, the Scarecrow, and the Cowardly Lion on the Yellow Brick Road. But this is *bad* method! One cannot simply take a secondary source (here, Acts) and derive from it a framework into which a primary source (here, Galatians) must be made to fit. The result of such harmonization is abusive of primary material and produces a distorted picture of early Christianity. But what is one to do? Here is a dilemma! Does one ignore the problem (many do), lose one's faith (some have), scoff at the veracity of the New Testament (some do), or wrestle with the problem and hope to come out like Jacob (in Genesis 32), altered but a winner?

Resolving Difficulties

There is a way to work through the rough spots in the reconstruction of Paul's life, but in order to do so, one must be guided by sound method. Briefly stated the method that will guide the remainder of this study is this:

1. The primary sources always have priority. Moreover, the soundest basis for understanding Paul is laid by using the seven undisputed letters of Paul: Romans, 1 Corinthians, 2 Corinthians, Galatians, Philippians, 1 Thessalonians, and Philemon. The other letters may be consulted in an ancillary capacity—though frankly, when consulted, they add little if anything to one's knowledge of Paul's life.

2. The secondary source, Acts, may be used cautiously as a supplement to the primary materials when it is not in conflict with the letters. Indeed, agreement of the primary and secondary materials gives one certainty, for the author of Acts shows no knowledge of Paul's letters or even that Paul wrote letters.

3. Other early Christian documents are almost useless for the purpose of reconstructing Paul's life. These works are highly legendary in character. But they do illustrate matters that are best regarded as *debatable* or *unknown*. For example, extrabiblical early Christian literature offers competing stories about Paul's death—some documents have him dying by execution in Rome at the conclusion of the im-

prisonment described in Acts; other stories claim he was set free and went to Spain; still others say he was set free, went to Spain, was again arrested and sent back to Rome where he was executed.

The Method Applied

By taking the autobiographical material in Paul's letters, comparing that information with Acts, and then considering the extrabiblical sources, one distinguishes two kinds of material. First, one isolates reliable information that allows one to compose Paul's story in outline. This is nothing like a biography, for the sources do not provide such extensive information; but one gets an impression of the man and develops a sketch of his career as an apostle. In the form of a sentence outline, the sketch appears as follows:

1. The man's name was Paul, a Greek name.
2. He had a Jewish name, Saul. (Having two names was not uncommon for Jews who lived outside Palestine in the first century.)
3. Paul was born in Tarsus, a city in southeastern Asia Minor.
4. He came from a family of Pharisees of the tribe of Benjamin and was named for the tribe's most illustrious member, King Saul.
5. Paul's letters show familiarity with both *rabbinic* methods for interpretation of scripture and *popular Hellenistic philosophy* to a degree that makes it likely he had formal education in both areas.
6. He was probably, as an adult, a resident of Damascus.
7. He was an active persecutor of the early Christian movement (probably because he perceived it to be a threat to Torah obedience).
8. Paul became a Christian, an apostle, through a dramatic *revelation* of Jesus Christ.
9. His first years as a Christian, spent in Arabia, are a mystery.
10. Three years after his call Paul went to Jerusalem to *visit*; he saw Peter and James.
11. Later (after fourteen years) he returned to Jerusalem for a meeting often referred to as "the Jerusalem Conference" or "the Apostolic Council."
12. Paul was a vigorous evangelist, traveling and preaching in Achaia,

Arabia, Asia, Cilicia, Galatia, Judea, Illyricum, Macedonia, and Syria, and making plans for Italy and Spain.

13. On the mission field he
    a. worked with a group of trusted colleagues (Aquila, Prisca, Silvanus, Sosthenes, Timothy, Titus, and others);
    b. supported himself with his craft, tentmaking;
    c. was often in danger and abused; and
    d. suffered from a "thorn in the flesh."
14. Along with evangelization, Paul worked among his non-Palestinian congregations on a major project, a collection for the "poor" in Jerusalem, which he hoped would reconcile the non-law-observant Christian givers and the law-observant Christian recipients.
15. While actively engaged in evangelization of a region, Paul wrote to churches he had founded earlier in other areas to address problems experienced by those congregations.
16. Paul's clear self-perception was that he was an "apostle of Jesus Christ to the Gentiles," i.e., one sent to proclaim the good news of Jesus Christ among non-Jews.
17. We lose sight of Paul in the primary sources as he is imprisoned in Caesarea writing to Philemon and to the church at Philippi. Nevertheless, with all but certainty we may conclude that while in prison (under Felix and then Festus), he appealed to be tried before Caesar (Nero) and was sent to Rome for a hearing. Subsequently, he died there as a martyr.

Even in this material there is some uncertainty. For example, because of the ambiguity of his statements, when Paul says "then after three years" (Gal 1:18) and "then after fourteen years" (Gal 2:1) one cannot be sure exactly what he means. He could be indicating two points in time, both dated from his call—to paraphrase, "then three years after my call" and "then fourteen years after my call." But he could mean "then three years after my call" and "then fourteen years later"—in other words, *seventeen* years. (Since Paul bases his argument in Galatians on the revelation of the risen Christ at his call, I prefer to understand both temporal references in relation to the time of the calling.)

A second kind of information isolated in this study is that information in the secondary sources about which the interpreters of Paul must express reservations. For example, Acts 22:3 informs the reader that Paul was brought up in Jerusalem at the feet of Gamaliel—in other words, Paul was a student in Jerusalem of one of the most famous rabbis in Jewish history. But Paul himself never mentions these credentials. This is striking, for there are places in his letters where he lists his "Jewish" credentials at length. The mention of Gamaliel in these listings would have amplified Paul's point concerning his former zeal for and status in Judaism, but he does not mention the connection. It is possible that Paul studied with Gamaliel in Jerusalem, but since he does not mention this himself, it is safest to omit this item when reconstructing his life.

Moreover, from Paul's own letters one would not gather that he was a resident of Jerusalem. Paul himself says he "went up to Jerusalem to visit" and that he "returned to Damascus" (Gal 1:18, 17). From this manner of reference, serious students of Paul's life and work understand that he was, as an adult, a resident of Damascus, not Jerusalem.

Even more problematic is the claim in Acts that Paul received an endorsement from the apostles in Jerusalem. Not only does Paul not say this, he flatly denies it in Galatians.

The standard scholarly explanation of these differences between Acts and Paul (as known from his letters) is expressed in terms of the known theological tendencies of the author of Acts, Luke. It is clear that Luke has an overarching concern to demonstrate the *continuity* of God's saving acts in human history. For him, Jerusalem itself is the center of God's past involvement with humanity; it is the center from which the gospel of Jesus Christ goes out. By bringing Paul to Jerusalem almost immediately after his conversion and by having him endorsed by the twelve apostles there, a linearity is shown to run from God, through Jesus Christ, through the apostles and the church in Jerusalem, to Paul and the churches he founded outside Palestine. In other words, Luke, writing in about A.D. 90, retells the story of earliest Christianity in order to document the continuity of the proclamation of the gospel and, thereby, to demonstrate the unity of the church in his own day.

In conclusion, by delineating and practicing a sound method for the use of sources in the reconstruction of Paul's life, one achieves valuable results. On the one hand, one exposes information that allows a more sophisticated reading of the New Testament documents in relation to one another. On the other, one develops a sketch of the life of Paul. This sketch may, through the conservatism of the method, be a minimal one; but it is absolutely reliable, admitting no debatable material. The sketch will be useful for the remainder of this study.

BIBLIOGRAPHY

G. Bornkamm, *Paul* (New York: Harper & Row, 1971).
J. C. Hurd, "Paul the Apostle," *IDBSup* 648–51.
J. Knox, *Chapters in a Life of Paul* (Nashville: Abingdon, 1950).
A. C. Purdy, "Paul the Apostle," *IDB* 3 681–704.

The World of Paul
and His Readers

Before attempting to trace Paul's career as an apostle in further detail, one needs to know something of the people among whom Paul worked, to whom he wrote, and the age in which they and the apostle lived. Without such basic information the modern reader of Paul's letters might find it impossible to cross the barriers of time (nearly 2,000 years), space (often thousands of miles), and culture (the high-tech West compared to the ancient East) and hear the apostle's words as did those to whom they were first addressed.

Paul and his original readers were citizens of the Roman Empire. While the Romans were the overlords of the period, the cultural heritage extended back to the earlier "Greeks." Thus, one speaks of Paul's world as *the Greco-Roman* or *Hellenistic* world, indicating a place where East and West had been brought together centuries earlier as part of the political vision of Alexander the Great (d. 323 B.C.). Alexander dreamed of ruling over a harmonious, unified world, and he believed that the way to achieve hegemony was to produce a culturally homogeneous population. Therefore, he sought to bring the diverse cultures and peoples of his empire together by disseminating ancient Greek thought, customs, and styles. This project is called Hellenization, and the synthesis of the Greek way of life with the customs of the other Mediterranean and Eastern cultures is called Hellenism. The vehicle for Alexander's project was the Greek city-state, or *polis*. He founded or refounded cities around the Mediterranean and well into Asia, imbuing these with the institutions of Greek cities. The dream was a grand one, and though Alexander and his successors (including even the Romans) were largely successful in implementing their strategy, for many reasons the dream proved to be an illusion.

In fact, by the time of Paul, there was widespread disillusionment throughout the Hellenistic world. Scholars debate the extent of this disenchantment. One commonly encountered phrase for describing the period refers to it as "an age of failure of nerve." This is an over-statement, but still one should realize that the "fullness of time" to which Paul refers (Gal 4:4) was a period of general anxiety. The age was characterized by extensive travel, rapid expansion of populations and cities, a questioning of the past and its values, and a searching for new answers.

The problems of Paul's world had their roots at least as far back as the third century B.C., a period of severe hardship in Greece itself. It had been a time of civil war that saw the demise of the Greek city-state and the near collapse of the civil judicial system. There had also been general famine, and the hardships were so severe as to motivate the practice of infanticide. In short, the Hellenistic dream of a world free from barbarism and corruption had rapidly devolved into a night-mare.

The social distress produced an atmosphere of universal cynicism. There was a loss of confidence in government and an accompanying loss of respect for other institutions. The world itself was suspected, and ways of thinking developed that genuinely devalued the *physical* and simultaneously elevated the *spiritual*. People longed for unseen things. The breakdown of society and the suspicion of things physical was reflected in the erosion of traditional, cultic, communal piety and the emergence of individual religion.

The population of the Hellenistic world responded in a variety of fashions to the dilemma. *Mystery religions* were popular. These were secretive organizations with private, elaborate rituals that emphasized the deification of mortals, namely those who were initiated into the mystery rites. The central concern of these organizations was with the personal salvation of the participants through the apprehension of the power associated with the various deities celebrated in the religions. For example, in the cult of Isis and Osiris, which began in Egypt and spread through the Mediterranean countries, the initiates dramatically reenacted the death and revivification of Osiris, the fraternal paramour of the earth goddess, Isis. By participating in the ritual of Osiris' murder and reanimation the participants believed they laid hold of the supernatural power that restored Osiris and, thereby, guaranteed their own immortality.

Other citizens of the Greco-Roman world attempted to deal with the Hellenistic malaise in what they considered a more rational fashion, namely through *philosophy*. In the first century several "schools" of philosophy claimed to have a line on "wisdom" that put the world into proper perspective. Among the better known philosophies were Stoicism, Cynicism, and Neo-Pythagoreanism. *Stoics* held that the world was ordered by the divine Logos. Therefore, all events fit some plan; and the human achieved true happiness, or well-being, by accepting the way things are. *Cynics* dealt with the world by recognizing the ephemeral quality of life, denouncing established convention, and practicing asceticism. They called for people to "know themselves," i.e., to come to self-realization through an awareness of the distinction between natural (nature's) and artificial (humanly created) values. *Neo-Pythagoreans* united philosophy and theology. They distinguished "soul" from "body" and taught that the divine soul was trapped in the body of all living things. On the principle that "like seeks like" they regarded the aim of life to be the stripping of the body so that the soul could return home to its source.

Also during the first century *Judaism* enjoyed some general popularity—though sadly, in the Greco-Roman era, as in other periods of history, there was widespread anti-Judaism (often commonly referred to by the misnomer, anti-Semitism). The reason for the favorable reception of Judaism by many non-Jews in the first century was that Judaism was perceived to be a pragmatic, sensible alternative to other religions and ways of thinking. Monotheism appealed to many first century urbanites as a cosmopolitan, sophisticated view of God. Moreover, the high moral standards of Judaism were attractive to many Hellenes. But, above all, Judaism offered hope by making God personal and human righteousness manageable through the system of Torah observance.

To make this clear, consider the broad pattern of Jewish religion in which the law functioned. Judaism rested on the twin pillars of *election* and *atonement*. In the first place, God chose (elected) Israel as his people. In relation to this election, the Torah (God's commandments, the law) was given to Israel. Israel kept the law as a response to God's election. It is important here to understand that Israel's keeping of the law was a *response* to her election, not a means to achieve salvation. Often Judaism is portrayed as a religion in which people kept the law in order to earn merit that won salvation for them. But this is a fundamental distortion of the role the law played in Judaism. To recapitulate: Judaism taught that God chose Israel and gave the law as the norm for Israel's response to his divine election. In other words, keeping the law was Israel's side of a bargain (covenant) God made with her. In the context of this covenant, Jews believed they were rewarded for their obedience and punished for their disobedience to the law. Moreover, Judaism provided for its adherents to make reparation for transgressions of the law, for Judaism had prescribed means of repentance in established acts of penitence for transgressors. Indeed, when the Jew faithfully performed the appropriate act of contrition, he or she was guaranteed that God would forgive the infelicity. In essence the pattern of Jewish religion was

ELECTION with

> *the law* as the normative response to God's choice, and *reward* for obedience and *punishment* for disobedience;

and

ATONEMENT

> through *repentance* and accompanying acts of contrition, bringing *forgiveness*.

Through this system Paul was able to say with confidence that he was "blameless" as a Jew (Phil 3:6). Without this understanding of "systemic righteousness" in first century Judaism modern readers of this claim conclude Paul was arrogant, a liar, or insane; with the information, however, Paul's statement becomes intelligible, and one can begin to understand the apostle.

BIBLIOGRAPHY

M. Hengel, *Judaism and Hellenism*, 2 vols. (Philadelphia: Fortress, 1974).

R. F. Hock, *The Social Context of Paul's Ministry* (Philadelphia: Fortress, 1980).

H. Koester, *Introduction to the New Testament*, Vol. 1, *History, Culture and Religion of the Hellenistic Age* (Philadelphia: Fortress, 1982).

E. Lohse, *The New Testament Environment* (Nashville: Abingdon, 1976).

W. A. Meeks, *The First Urban Christians* (New Haven: Yale, 1983).

F. E. Peters, *The Harvest of Hellenism* (New York: Touchstone, 1970).

B. Reicke, *The New Testament Era* (Philadelphia: Fortress, 1968).

E. P. Sanders, *Paul and Palestinian Judaism* (Philadelphia: Fortress, 1977).

Paul's Background and Christian Point of Departure

In order to understand people, it is almost necessary to know "where they are coming from" and "what they are getting at." Paul is no exception. Paul the Christian had once been Paul (Saul) the Jew. It is clear from both his own letters and the story of his ministry in Acts that Paul was once not merely a Jew but a Pharisee. He boasts from time to time in his letters of his Jewish past in rebuttal to other missionaries who caused problems in the churches that he had founded (see Phil 3 and 2 Cor 11). In so doing, Paul reveals that prior to being a Christian he was a zealous Pharisee. Acts 22:3 preserves a tradition that associates Paul with Rabbi Gamaliel I, one of the most influential figures in first century Judaism. Independent from this memory (we saw earlier that Paul does not mention this striking association when rehearsing his Jewish credentials), the association of Paul with formal rabbinic education seems likely, for in his writings Paul manifests signs of "rabbinics": he does midrashic exegesis of the Old Testament, he demonstrates a clear perception of the law as the heart of Judaism, and the contrast he draws between Christ and the law shows his disavowal of human, systemic righteousness which he had once practiced with confidence and contentment. These features of Paul's writings locate him within the stream of first century Pharisaic Judaism; they do not, however, amount to evidence for the assertion that Paul was a rabbi.

As it is clear that Paul's past was in Pharisaic Judaism, it is also certain that Paul was a Hellenized Jew. According to Acts he was born outside Palestine in the Greco-Roman trade city of Tarsus. Indeed,

Paul's own writings show signs of Hellenistic education. The basic mastery of the skills of reading, thinking, argumentation, and expression in writing are the hallmarks of Hellenistic education. Moreover, the letters are filled with telltale signs of Paul's Hellenistic heritage. From his quotations of the Old Testament one sees that Paul read the scriptures in their Greek version, the Septuagint. Paul is thoroughly familiar with the conventions of popular Hellenistic philosophy and methods of literary interpretation. Moreover, he calls himself *Paul* (Greek, *Paulos*), not *Saul* (Hebrew, *Sā'ûl*), and his metaphors are drawn from the Greco-Roman world of sports and military.

These observations illustrate a basic problem for those seeking to understand Paul—namely, what background best accounts for Paul's own understanding of what he did and said? Formerly scholars drew hard lines between three areas that putatively influenced Paul. Since he was certainly a Pharisee, *rabbinic Judaism* was thought to provide *the* key to interpreting Paul. His use of apparently technical language in reference to tradition he had *received* and *delivered* (1 Cor 15:3) to the churches he founded was taken to indicate his self-understanding and his attitude toward the tradition itself. Moreover, Paul's practice of midrashic exegesis (see Paul on Exodus in 1 Cor 10) was thought to reveal his approach to the Old Testament, while his concern with the contrast between Christ and the law was determined by his past participation in Pharisaism.

Yet, other scholars argued that *Hellenism* was the most appropriate background for viewing and interpreting Paul. That Paul did allegorical exegesis was said to show still another attitude and approach toward the Old Testament (see Paul on Sarah and Hagar in Gal 4). Furthermore, it was held that by casting Paul in the context of Hellenism one found the prerequisite clues for understanding such basic Pauline notions as the sacraments and Christology. Since Paul was thoroughly Hellenistic in heritage, this meant that he would interpret baptism and the Lord's Supper in relation to the practices of Hellenistic mystery religions, and he would have understood Christ in terms of a general, Hellenistic myth of a descending and ascending redeemer figure.

A third approach to Paul designated *apocalyptic Judaism* as the determinative background for understanding his writings. Paul's language bespeaks an apocalyptic perspective in focusing on wrath, judgment, and the day of the Lord. He displays a yearning for the messianic age that characterized all apocalyptic writing. He shows an awareness of living at the juncture of two ages, one dying and one being born. Further, he has a sense of special urgency derived from the apocalyptic conviction that his generation is the last. And the clearest sign of Paul's thoroughly apocalyptic perspective is the presence in his writings of the *dualistic* doctrine of two ages that recognized no continuity between this world and the world to come. This doctrine maintains that the age to come breaks into the current age supernaturally through God's intervention and without human agency. This description of apocalyptic thought brings to mind 1 Cor 10:11, where Paul speaks of himself and others as those "upon whom *the ends of the ages* have met" (notice the double plural mistranslated by most modern English versions).

Scholars now recognize that one cannot draw hard lines between these three areas of influence. Rather, those seeking to understand Paul must weigh his statements in relation to each of these backgrounds, for Paul was influenced by and drew from all of them. Nevertheless, the question remains whether one of these areas is dominant. In the course of examining Paul's letters and in pondering his theology, one is able to see that all that Paul did and wrote hangs together on the essential framework of apocalyptically patterned thought. This topic will be discussed again in this chapter as a key to Paul's thought and in a more extensive fashion in the chapter on Paul's theology.

Paul's Pre-Christian Activity

Both Paul and Acts indicate that before he was a Christian Paul was a persecutor of the adherents of the early Christian movement. As Helmut Koester has observed, however, "it is difficult to imagine Paul's primary [pre-Christian] profession was that of an itinerant persecutor of Christians." From Acts one learns that as a Christian missionary Paul practiced the trade of tentmaking in order to support himself on the mission field. Perhaps he also made tents before he was a Christian, for he would have received training in his trade as a youth. But what would have motivated a Jewish tentmaker, even a pious one, to engage in persecution of those who claimed that Jesus was the Messiah? The answer to this question may provide us with some insight into Paul's immediate pre-Christian activity. In moving toward an answer it is necessary to gather information about the Hellenistic, synagogue Judaism from which Paul came and the relationship between that expression of Judaism and the earliest Christians.

Careful, extensive work has demonstrated that diaspora (Hellenistic, non-Palestinian, synagogue) Judaism paved the way for earliest Christian missionary proclamation of the gospel. Traditionally Christians (and even some Jews) think of first century Judaism as an exclusive religion, and for certain sectarian Jews, like the Essenes of the Qumran community at the Dead Sea, this impression is accurate. But all first century Jews, even all Palestinian Jews, were no more hardline separatists than all contemporary Jews are of the Hasidic persuasion. Indeed, Hellenistic, synagogue Judaism seems to have engaged in lively missionary activity in an effort to convert Gentiles to Judaism. The missionary activity of the synagogues was apparently successful, for there is archaeological and literary evidence of both Gentiles, called "proselytes," who became full converts to Judaism and Gentiles who formally associated themselves with the synagogue as "God-fearers" but who did not become full participants by undergoing circumcision. Both groups were attracted to the high moral standards of the systemic righteousness that claimed to make God personal and salvation possible.

The law was the key to Jewish missionary activity. It was the means by which one and all participated in the salvific covenant with God. Thus, it was a natural reaction on the part of Judaism to combat any threat to the law. Early Christianity with its proclamation of a crucified Messiah posed not only a threat in competing for converts within and without the synagogue, it proclaimed an absolute contrast between Messiah and law. A Messiah who died by crucifixion, cursed under the law, was irreconcilable with the law that issued the curse. Paul the Christian, reflecting upon the relationship between Christ and the law, saw this sheer incompatibility as clearly as did anyone in the first century.

By examining the evidence available, it seems not only reasonable, but likely, that *before he was a Christian missionary (apostle) Paul was a Jewish missionary in behalf of the synagogue mission to the Gentiles*. First, that Paul the Christian saw clearly the absolute incompatibility of salvation through the crucified Christ with salvation through the law may mean that Paul the Jew saw the same conflict and was thereby motivated to engage in persecution of the Christians. Paul's former devotion to practice of the law does not itself explain his zeal in persecuting the Christian movement, for many early Christians were content both to confess Jesus as Messiah and to engage in law-observant living. There is ample evidence of such Jewish Christians (or, Christian Jews) in Paul's letters and in the rest of the New Testament. The most famous example of this type of Christian is James, the brother of Jesus, who was a key figure in the life of the church in Jerusalem. Early Christianity preserves an image of him as one zealously devoted to observing the law. Though late (c. A.D. 325) and legendary in character, a description of James in an early history of the church illustrates this point:

> The charge of the church passed to James the brother of the Lord, together with the apostles. He was called the "Just" by all men from the Lord's time to ours, since many are called James but he was holy from his mother's womb. He drank no wine or strong drink, nor did he eat flesh; no razor went upon his head; he did not anoint himself with oil, and he did not go to the baths. He alone was allowed to enter into the sanctuary, for he did not wear wool but linen, and he used to enter alone into the temple and be found kneeling and praying for forgiveness for the people, so that his knees grew hard like a camel's because of his constant worship of God, kneeling and asking forgiveness for the people. So from his excessive righteousness he was called the Just and Oblias, that is in Greek, "Rampart of the people and righteous" as the prophets declare concerning him (from Eusebius, *Ecclesiastical History* 2.23.4–7, citing Hegesippus).

Thus, one sees that Paul's recognition of the contrary nature of salvation through Christ and salvation through the law was not a necessary part of his becoming a Christian. Others perceived no conflict, but harmony, between Christ and the law.

Perhaps it was Paul's perception of conflict and his own pre-Christian activity as a Jewish missionary that motivated his persecution of Christians. This seems possible, even reasonable, but one striking piece of evidence makes this conclusion almost certain. At Gal 5:11, Paul says, "But if I, brothers and sisters, still preach circumcision, why am I still persecuted?" Paul the former persecutor is now himself persecuted because he does not *still* preach circumcision. When did Paul ever preach circumcision? There is no evidence that Paul the Christian ever did so, but the evidence examined indicates that Paul the Jew may have done so; indeed, in light of the full evidence, he likely did so.

Paul's So-Called Conversion

People frequently speak of Paul's conversion from Judaism to Christianity, but the apostle himself refrains from describing his experience in this way. By his own account, Paul's experience was less a conversion than a *prophetic call*. At Gal 1:15–16 Paul sounds more like the opening verses of Jeremiah (1:4–10) than a description of one's conversion from one religion to another:

Paul: "[God] who had set me apart from my mother's womb, and had called me through his grace, was pleased to reveal his Son to me, in order that I might preach him among the Gentiles (or, nations)."

Jeremiah: "Now the word of the Lord came to me saying, 'Before I formed you in the womb I knew you, and before you were born I consecrated you; I appointed you a prophet to the nations.' "

Moreover, there is no evidence in Paul's writings that he experienced disillusionment with his past life in Judaism. When necessary he can and does speak about his past with pride, as he does in Galatians (1:14), Philippians (3:4–11), and 2 Corinthians (11:21–22). Indeed, in reflecting upon his Jewish past, Paul is able to regard it as a former *gain* that is now a *loss* (Phil 3:7–8). Furthermore, there is no evidence that Paul the Jew had a painful (or other!) consciousness of sin; in fact, he is able to say that he was "blameless" in his Jewish life under the law. What Paul the Christian evinces is *a new perspective from which he simply rejects his past,* though not bitterly. He claims that, based upon God's revelation to him of Jesus Christ, he came to regard his former life in Judaism as a loss. Understanding the absolute conflict between the crucified Christ and the law and having had the risen Christ revealed to him by God, Paul was called to be an apostle to the Gentiles. Inherent in the call were both a repudiation of Paul's religious past and a reorientation toward Christ that set the course of Paul's entire life as a Christian.

Indeed Paul understood his calling as a divine commissioning as an *apostle* (literally, "one who is sent") to the Gentiles. This basic insight provides important aid for following the line of Paul's argumentation in several of his letters. On occasions during his ministry questions were raised about the gospel Paul preached and the legitimacy of his apostleship. This happened dramatically in Galatia and Corinth. When such questions were raised Paul came back fighting tooth and nail. At first consideration one might think Paul defensive for merely egotistical reasons, but reflection upon Paul's defensive arguments in light of his statements about his call exposes a different motivation: Paul defended his *message* and his *apostleship* because both extended from his *call*, which was the result of the *revelation* of the risen Jesus Christ to him, which was an act of *God*. Thus to question Paul's gospel or his apostleship was to question his call; and to question his call was to question the revelation of the risen Lord; and to question that revelation was to question God! Paul usually responded to his critics by arguing at the level of the nature of the gospel or the legitimacy of his apostleship, but, when pushed, Paul would resort to arguments about God, as he does in Gal 3:19–20.

BIBLIOGRAPHY

J. C. Beker, *Paul's Apocalyptic Gospel* (Philadelphia: Fortress, 1982).

R. Bultmann, *Theology of the New Testament,* 2 vols. (New York: Scribner's Sons, 1951/1955).

W. D. Davies, *Paul and Rabbinic Judaism* (4th ed.; Philadelphia: Fortress, 1980—1st ed., 1948).

E. Käsemann, "Justification and Salvation History in the Epistle to the Romans" in his *Perspectives on Paul* (Philadelphia: Fortress, 1971) 60–78.

J. L. Martyn, "Epistemology at the Turn of the Ages: 2 Corinthians 5:16" in W. R. Farmer, C. F. D. Moule, and R. R. Niebuhr, eds., *Christian History and Interpretation* (Cambridge: University Press, 1967) 267–87.

K. Stendahl, *Paul among Jews and Gentiles* (Philadelphia: Fortress, 1976).

Paul at Work

In his letters Paul frequently refers to himself as an "apostle" (Rom 1:1; 1 Cor 1:1; 2 Cor 1:1; Gal 1:1). The noun *apostle* (*apostolos* in Greek) derives from a verb that means "to send" (*apostellein* in Greek). This was Paul's self-understanding, that *he had been called in order to be sent.* And go he did, throughout the world he knew, preaching the "good news" of what God had done and was doing through Jesus Christ.

Paul's Basic Proclamation

For Paul, the gospel was indicative not imperative. His message was a proclamation of the powerful grace of God that was revealed in the Crucified and Resurrected One. He boldly announced that "God was in Christ reconciling the world to himself, not counting their trespasses against them" (2 Cor 5:19). He did not, in the style of an eighteenth century revivalist, say, "Jesus did it. Come and get it." Paul's gospel was not a proclamation coupled with an admonition; rather, it was the straightforward announcement of God's saving activity in Jesus Christ.

The message was directed toward human listeners, but it was not "news" they were to ponder and to which they might respond or not. Paul announced the all-sufficient divine act, the death and resurrection of Jesus, that simultaneously saved humanity and revealed the power of God that did the saving. Some listeners heard the message and believed, and, perceiving themselves saved by a gracious and powerful God, they lived transformed lives (1 Thess 1:2–10). Others heard and believed Paul's preaching, but for one reason or another they mis-

27

understood Paul's announcement of their "freedom" (see esp. 1 and 2 Corinthians). Still others heard and did not believe, sometimes not merely denying Paul's message but also opposing his ministry (2 Cor 11:12–15; 1 Thess 2:13–16). These varying receptions of Paul and his message will be examined in detail in the study of Paul's letters below. For now, one needs a clearer understanding of the missionary style of the apostle.

Paul's Missionary Technique

Toward the end of his ministry Paul says, "I have been able to bring to completion [the preaching of] the gospel of Christ from Jerusalem around as far as Illyricum" (Rom 15:19). In modern terms he claims to have preached the "good news" from Israel through Lebanon, Syria, Turkey, and Greece, as far as portions of Bulgaria, Albania, and Yugoslavia. How could Paul have done this in twenty to twenty-five years of his ministry?

The usual image of Paul is of a shrewd, energetic, tenacious, individual preacher, but one should recognize that Paul's missionary activity was *team work*. His letters reveal that he coordinated the activity of a systematically organized band of missionaries and that his method was fairly consistent.

Paul would move with a group of seasoned missionary colleagues to the capital city of a Roman province. Upon arrival he and his associates would approach the local synagogue, and if possible set up a base therein for the proclamation of the gospel. If no synagogue existed, the team would seek out the "God-fearers," i.e., Gentiles who were attracted to the theology and morality of Judaism but who had not become full converts. If there were no God-fearers, Paul and his companions would take the message to the local marketplace. In the process of moving into a city Paul would gather any Christians who already lived there and incorporate them into the missionary enterprise, thereby expanding his staff. While Paul seems to have remained in the capital city and its immediate area, his fellow workers appear to have dispersed themselves throughout the other cities, towns, and villages of the region in order to establish satellite congregations. Paul would remain in one location until the job he set out to do was done (he was in Corinth a year and a half and in Ephesus two years and three months) or, more often, until he became embroiled in a controversy that forced him to leave the region.

Paul then moved on to repeat this process in a new location. But, he did not lose contact with the churches he founded. Indeed, he paid checkup visits to the churches when he deemed it necessary. Moreover, he used the writing of letters as a part of his missionary strategy, employing the written communication (like a modern "bishop's letter") to influence and build up the congregations he addressed.

Some scholars attribute this method of organizing missionary work to the church at Antioch of which Paul was a member, and which itself was extremely active in early Christian missionary work. This may be the case; or, if Paul was a Jewish missionary before he was a Christian, perhaps he adapted the technique from Jewish missionary activity It may even be that Paul devised the strategy himself. Knowing the source of Paul's missionary style would be enlightening, but not knowing this does not detract from understanding Paul's work and appreciating its effectiveness.

Paul the Letter Writer

Since Paul's letters are what remain directly from his labors as an apostle, one should examine them in terms of their organization and style to see if they offer further insight into the character of their author. To perceive the genius of Paul's letters it is helpful to know something about letters and letter writing in antiquity.

Education, commerce, and travel in the Hellenistic era created a context for letter writing. There was even a semi-professional class of letter writers called *scribes* or the *amanuenses*. Letters moved surprising distances in Paul's day. The first "traveling" letters were official communications regarding governmental and military matters, but with improved conditions all sorts of letters were produced. These included public decrees by rulers, official letters between authorities, business letters, friendly communications, and brief notes of all sorts.

In Paul's day, as today, letters were written in standard forms. A brief letter from a man named Irenaeus to his brother Apollinarius is one of the best known examples of the form of a Hellenistic letter.

Irenaeus to Apollinarius, his dearest brother, many greetings. I pray continually for your health, and I myself am well. I wish you to know that I reached land on the sixth of the month Epeiph and we unloaded our cargo on the eighteenth of the same month. I went up to Rome, on the twenty-fifth of the same month, and the place welcomed us as the god willed, and we are daily expecting our discharge, it being that up till today nobody in the corn fleet has been released. Many salutations to your wife and to Serenus and to all who love you, each by name. Goodbye. Mesore 9.

To Apollinarius from his brother Irenaeus.

Notice the five sections of the standard letter: (1) a *salutation* in three parts which names the sender and the addressee and offers a greeting; (2) a *thanksgiving*; (3) the *body* of the letter; (4) *final instructions (parenesis)* (missing here); (5) the *closing* in two parts which offers final greetings and the parting word. The letter is also dated and addressed.

It is instructive to compare Paul's briefest letter, Philemon, as an example of Paul's letter writing style, with Irenaeus' letter. When this is done, one readily recognizes that the letters are remarkably similar in structure. Indeed, Paul's letter has the same five parts found in a standard letter.

1. Salutation

Sender(s):
"Paul, a prisoner of Christ Jesus and Timothy our brother"

Recipient(s):
"to Philemon our beloved fellow worker and Apphia our sister and Archippus our fellow soldier and the church in your house"

Greeting:
"Grace to you and peace from God our Father and the Lord Jesus Christ"

2. Thanksgiving

"I thank my God always when I remember you (singular, indicating Philemon) in my prayers"

3. Body of the Letter

Paul discusses the return of Onesimus, a runaway slave.

4. Final Instructions (Parenesis)

Throughout the letter Paul has exhorted Philemon:
"receive him" (v. 17)
"charge that to my account" (v. 18)
"refresh my heart in Christ" (v. 20)
His final instructions are in v. 22,
"prepare a guest room for me."

5. Closing

Greetings:
"Epaphras, my fellow prisoner in Christ Jesus, greets you (singular) [and] Mark, Aristarchus, Demas, and Luke, my fellow workers"
Parting word:
"The grace of the Lord Jesus Christ be with your spirit"

As similar as the letters of Paul and Irenaeus are, one should notice how Paul subtly altered the style of the standard Hellenistic letter for his own purposes. These alterations reflect the peculiarly Christian character of Paul's letters and reveal how thoroughly his relationship with Jesus Christ affected him. Indeed, God's revelation of the risen Christ gave Paul a new emphasis and left its stamp on everything he did, even the writing of letters.

To understand Paul's new emphasis it is helpful to view the anatomy of some of Paul's changes of the form of a standard letter. For example, *in the opening* of his letters Paul identifies himself in relation to God and Christ. Moreover, he identifies those to whom he writes in terms of their own roles as Christians. Furthermore, he alters the language of the normal greeting and expands it into a lofty but practical wish for the recipients. The usual salutation in Hellenistic letters is the word *greetings*. But Paul does not send his readers "greetings"; he salutes them by saying, "grace and peace." The words *greetings* and *grace* resemble one another in Greek: "greetings" = *chairein* and "grace" = *charis*. Thus, Paul's salutation begins with a wordplay that reveals the effects of God's activity, and he develops his altered greeting by coupling a common Jewish greeting, "peace" (*shalom*), with "grace."

In conclusion one should recognize that Paul was not a casual letter writer. His are not simple friendly communications. He wrote to address specific situations that existed in particular churches. With his letters he sought to extend his influence (often in an authoritative fashion) in order to assure desired results. He always strives to build up the congregation addressed. Thus, for Paul *the letter was an instrument of his apostleship*.

BIBLIOGRAPHY

For the text of the letter of Irenaeus see *B.G.U.* 27, cited here from C. K. Barrett, ed., *The New Testament Background: Selected Documents* (New York: Harper & Row, 1956).

For further information:

W. G. Doty, *Letters in Primitive Christianity* (Philadelphia: Fortress, 1973).

H. Koester, *Introduction to the New Testament,* Vol. 2, *History and Literature of Early Christianity* (Philadelphia: Fortress, 1982).

W. Schmithals, *The Office of Apostle in the Early Church* (Nashville: Abingdon, 1969).

J. H. Schütz, *Paul and the Anatomy of Apostolic Authority* (SNTSMS 26; Cambridge: University Press, 1975).

Tracing Paul's Travels and Work

The overview of Paul's life and work to this point has been a general one, developed thematically. Having considered the foregoing material, one is now prepared to turn to specifics—to times and places—in order to map a Pauline chronology.

But immediately one finds a lack of real detail for the task. Moreover, even with regard to some of the available details there are uncertainties. We recognized the problem of how to understand Paul's references to "three" and "fourteen" years above, and similar ambiguities exist for other statements. For example, how long was Paul in Arabia (Gal 1:17)? Or when he writes in Philippians and Philemon that he is in prison, where is he? And when he says he is confident of his impending release, is he merely being optimistic? Or does he have some reason to believe he will be freed? Or is he playing a bluff to motivate those to whom he writes?

Because of the lack of specific information and in light of the difficulties associated with using what material is available, many scholars argue that no more than a relative dating of Paul's letters is possible. And even here there are problems, for the preserved copies of Paul's letters are not dated. Moreover, the claims of some scholars to recognize developments in Paul's thinking from one letter to another are not persuasive, being locked in as they are to the presuppositions that Paul's thought evolved and that he could not change his mind.

From these cautionary remarks one might gather that the prospect of working out a Pauline chronology is bleak. But these warnings should not completely deter an attempt at correlating dates and places for Paul's career. Indeed, one firm date for Paul's activity is ascertainable. From Acts 18:12–18 one learns that Paul was in Corinth when Gallio was proconsul. An inscription found at Delphi (an ancient Greek town) permits dating of Gallio's term as proconsul to the period from May of A.D. 51 to May of A.D. 52. By correlating Acts and the Delphic inscription, one learns when Paul could possibly have appeared before Gallio. At the earliest it was the summer of 51 and at the latest the spring of 52. Scholars mount arguments for both extremities, but they have not resolved the issue which is perhaps unresolvable. Since there is nothing in Acts 18:12 to indicate that Gallio had taken office only recently (Acts 18:11 is a simple atemporal summary and does not indicate past time), for convenience we will settle on the later date—though recognizing that one may adjust the ensuing reconstruction by moving back the dates almost one year.

The information concerning Paul's imprisonment in Caesarea under Felix and then Festus is another "definite" moment in Paul's life. Some scholars correlate the information in Acts 24–26 with other material from Roman history concerning the family of Felix, but this is quite complicated and the case is fraught with difficulties, even improbabilities, and is merely speculative. Thus it is best to use the information in Paul's letters and Acts to work forward and backward from the dating of Gallio's proconsulship. Also to be considered are the conditions for travel in the ancient Greek world. For example, those who traveled on foot, as Paul no doubt did, could cover about twenty miles per day; few sea voyages took place during March, April, May, September, and October, and from November through February the Mediterranean was effectively closed for travel. Taking all these factors into the calculation, one achieves the following chronological outline:

A CHRONOLOGY OF PAUL'S MINISTRY

35 (or 32)	Paul is called by God's revelation of Jesus Christ (problem of "three" and "fourteen")
35–38	missionary activity in ARABIA (Gal 1:17) and DAMASCUS (2 Cor 11:32)
38	Paul visits with Peter (and James) in JERUSALEM (Gal 1:18)
38–48	missionary activity in CILICIA & SYRIA (Gal 1:21)
48	so-called Apostolic Council in JERUSALEM (Gal 2:1–10; Acts 15)
48 or 49	incident with Peter and others in ANTIOCH (Gal 2:11–14)
49	missionary activity in GALATIA (Acts 16:6)

A CHRONOLOGY OF PAUL'S MINISTRY (*Continued*)

50	missionary activity in PHILIPPI, THESSALONICA, & BEROEA (Acts 16:11–17:14)

Late 50   travel to CORINTH via ATHENS (Acts 17.15, 18.1), WRITING OF 1 THESSALONIANS

Late 50 to May 52
    missionary activity in CORINTH (Acts 18:11)

Summer 52
    travel to CAESAREA; then ANTIOCH; then passing through ASIA MINOR he paid a second visit to GALATIA on the way to EPHESUS (Gal 4:13; Acts 18:18–23)

Late 52 to spring 55
    missionary activity in EPHESUS (Acts 19:1, 8–10, 22); **WRITING OF GALATIANS, 2 COR 6.14–7.1, 1 CORINTHIANS, AND THE LETTERS PRESERVED IN 2 COR 8 AND 2:14–6:13; 7:2–4**

(54)   visit to CORINTH
    (presupposed in 2 Cor 13.1)

(Late 54–55)
    WRITING OF LETTER PRESERVED IN 2 COR 10–13

Summer 55
    travel through MACEDONIA to CORINTH; **WRITING OF LETTER PRESERVED IN 2 COR 1:1–2:13; 7:5–16; AND OF THE FINAL "COLLECTION LETTER," 2 COR 9**

Late 55-early 56
    stay in CORINTH; **WRITING OF ROMANS**

56   travel to JERUSALEM with the collection; arrest and imprisonment

56–58   imprisonment in CAESAREA; **WRITING OF PHILIPPIANS AND PHILEMON**

58   Felix replaced by Festus; Paul appeals to Caesar and is sent to ROME

58–60   imprisonment in ROME (Acts 28:30)

60+   martyrdom

This scheme outlines the major movements and the writing of Paul's letters and it will guide the course of the subsequent study of Paul's letters. These will be considered in the order of writing suggested in this chronology. In the introduction to each of the letters considered below, I give explicit reasons for locating the letters as they are situated temporally and geographically in this outline.

The conclusion that Paul did not write the six disputed letters lies behind this particular reconstruction. The decisions concerning the authorship of these letters are not related to chronology, however; and those who conclude that Paul did write the disputed letters can easily factor their conclusions into this account of Paul's life by locating 2 Thessalonians shortly after 1 Thessalonians, late in A.D. 50 or early in 51 from Corinth. Furthermore, most scholars who accept Colossians, Ephesians, and the pastoral epistles as authentic Pauline letters usually and most aptly regard them as coming from the time of Paul's Roman imprisonment. If one concludes that any or all of these are genuine Pauline correspondences, one may set the letter(s) in the period A.D. 58–60 + .

BIBLIOGRAPHY

J. C. Hurd, "Chronology, Pauline," *IDBSup* 166–67.

R. Jewett, *A Chronology of Paul's Life* (Philadelphia: Fortress, 1979).

J. Knox, *Chapters in a Life of Paul* (Nashville: Abingdon, 1950).

G. Luedemann, *Paul, Apostle to the Gentiles* (Philadelphia: Fortress, 1984—German original 1980).

Finding a Key to Paul's Thought

Before concluding this consideration of Paul *the man,* we should ask about the mind of the apostle. This is a vital point since whatever one presupposes on this matter informs the way one reads Paul's letters and, in turn, how one understands Paul's theology. The goal here is not to psychologize Paul—many such attempts have been made and all are splendid failures. Rather we seek the key to Paul's understanding of Christianity. The search for this key is similar to launching a quest for the Holy Grail, for one could devote a lifetime to this topic (many scholars have) and still not resolve the matter to the liking of all students of Paul.

We saw above that individual cases can and have been made for rabbinic Judaism, Hellenism, and apocalyptic Judaism as "the most appropriate background against which to view Paul." Today scholars correctly recognize that these backgrounds are not exclusive of one another and that each makes a contribution to a balanced reading of Paul, but it is becoming increasingly clear through the work of several contemporary scholars (see the writings of Beker, Käsemann, and Martyn in the bibliography) that the *apocalyptic* element provided Paul with the basic framework of his thought and determined his comprehension of the world around him. What is this *apocalyptic perspective*? Since a variety of understandings of "apocalyptic" exist, what follows is an explanation of the meaning of *apocalyptic* in this book.

In Greek *apokalypsis* means "revelation." Paul uses this word to refer to his original encounter with the risen Jesus Christ (Gal 1:13). That dramatic revelation was the occasion of Paul's call. Moreover, it was the time and means of Paul's being taught or given the basis of the gospel which he preached (Gal 1:11–17). This disruptive inter-

vention of God into Paul's life bespeaks the pattern of thought typical
of first century apocalyptic Judaism.

Apocalyptic is a special expression of Jewish *eschatology* that was
characterized by the *dualistic* doctrine of two ages. On the one hand
there is "the present evil age," and on the other there is "the age to
come." The "present evil age" is the world of mundane realities in
which human beings live; the "age to come" is the supernatural realm
of the power of God. There is no continuity between these ages. Indeed, apocalyptic Jewish thought held that at some future moment "the
age to come" would break into the human realm by a supernatural act
of God. In this moment of God's intervention the "present evil age"
would pass away and "the age to come" would be established as a
new reality, ordained and directed by God. Apocalyptic Judaism held
that by this act of God evil would be annihilated and those who were
righteous would be redeemed. Thus "the age to come" was the hope
of those who believed in God but found themselves oppressed by the
forces of evil in the present world. In Jewish apocalyptic literature the
authors usually claim to live in the last days of "the present evil age."
Their message to readers is the joint promise and warning that the
intervention of God is about to happen.

Throughout his letters Paul's language and patterns of thought
reveal elements of this apocalyptic eschatology. For example, Paul
frequently uses apocalyptic language: "destined . . . for wrath," "the
wrath to come," "the wrath of God," "the day of wrath," "the day of
the Lord Jesus Christ," "the day of salvation," "redeemed," "redemption," "this age," "the rulers of this age," "the present evil age," and
"the ends of the ages." Moreover, Paul reveals in his letters the conviction that he and his readers are part of the last generation of humanity (1 Thess 4:13–18, esp. v. 17; 1 Cor 15:51–57).

Paul does not use the phrase "the age to come," and so some
scholars deny the thoroughgoing apocalyptic character of his thought.
But he speaks in distinctively Christian phrases of the same idea when
he says "a new creation" and "the kingdom of God." This alteration
of phrases indicates a slight, but fundamental, alteration on the part
of Paul. He transforms the pattern of Jewish apocalyptic thought described above into a particularly Christian pattern of apocalyptic thinking which permeates all of his writings. In other words, *Paul the*

*apostle articulates an apocalyptic perspective that has been modified
in light of the Christ-event.*

Jewish apocalyptic eschatology thought in terms of two ages.
These were distinct; one age ended and the other began by an inter-
vening act of God. The following diagram illustrates this mind-set:

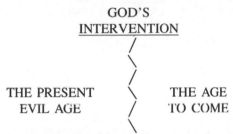

GOD'S
INTERVENTION

THE PRESENT   THE AGE
EVIL AGE   TO COME

Paul has a similar, but distinct, view of time that stamps his entire
thought process. He maintains the temporal dualism characteristic of
Jewish apocalyptic, but he modifies the scheme in light of the Christ-
event so that there are two distinct ages that are separated and joined
by an interim.

For Paul the first temporal epoch is "the present evil age" (Gal
1:4; 1 Cor 2:6–8). This age is ruled by the god of this world (2 Cor
4:4), namely Satan, and by the elemental spirits of the universe (Gal
4:3; 1 Cor 2:8). Under the influence of its rulers this age is at odds
with God (1 Cor 15:24–28; Rom 8:37–39). Nevertheless, this age is
passing away (1 Cor 7:31).

The second epoch is the "new creation" (Gal 6:14; 2 Cor 5:17).
This new age comes as God in Christ defeats the forces in opposition
to him (Gal 6:14; 1 Cor 7:31; Rom 5:21), and it is established as the
regnum Dei, apparently an age of glory (1 Thess 2:10–12; 1 Cor
15:20–28; 2 Cor 4:17; Rom 5:2, 21).

The *present* exists as the juncture of the ages or as a mingling
of the ages (1 Cor 10:11; 2 Cor 5:16). Here 1 Cor 10:11 is important.
In this verse Paul describes himself and other humans as those *eis
hous ta telē tōn aiōnōn katentēken.* Modern translations often obscure
Paul's idea in this phrase, translating it as does the RSV, "upon whom
the end of the ages has come." This rendering implies that Paul stands
at the end of time and looks back at the ages (something like dispen-

sations?) that have gone before—indeed, he does not. The phrase literally says, "upon whom the end*s* of the age*s* have met." Paul perceives that he and other humans live at the juncture of the ages. This
juncture came about as a result of the cross of Christ (1 Cor 1:17–
18) and it will conclude, marking the absolute end of the present evil
age, at the coming of Christ from heaven (1 Thess 2:19; 3:13; 4:13–
18; 1 Cor 15:23–28). Again, a diagram illustrates the matter:

GOD'S INTERVENTION IN:

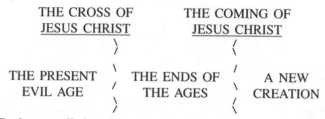

Paul was called and he thought, worked, and preached in this
interim. Much of Paul's message derives from his understanding of
this juncture, for, as noted, it came about as a result of the cross of
Christ (1 Cor 1:17–18). In essence Paul said:

1. Sin has been defeated (Gal 1:4; 1 Cor 15:3; Rom 4:25).
2. Death has been condemned (1 Cor 15:54–57; Rom 8:31–39).
3. The law has been exposed for what it is (Gal 3:24–25; Rom 7:7–
   12).
4. Christ has discharged humanity from the curse of the law (Gal
   3:13–14; Rom 7:4–6).
5. Although the battle goes on toward God's final victory, creation
   has been reclaimed by God (1 Cor 15:20–28; Rom 8:18–25).
6. God's sovereignty has been established (Rom 8:31–39).
7. Creation presently awaits the grand assize (1 Thess 5:2–11; 1 Cor
   6:2–3; 15:20–28; 16:21; Rom 8:18–25), and while the kingdom
   of God has *not yet* been fully established in glory, this is *already*
   the Messianic age in which, for now, everything is to be viewed
   from the vantage point of the cross (2 Cor 5:16).

The thesis that Paul was an *apocalyptic* thinker informs the remainder of this study. The validity of this thoroughly apocalyptic understanding of Paul will be demonstrated as "apocalyptic" successfully provides interpretative insights into Paul's thinking. Indeed, that this framework was the one in relation to which Paul thought will become increasingly clear as the letters are examined.

BIBLIOGRAPHY

J. C. Beker, *Paul the Apostle* (2d ed.; Philadelphia: Fortress, 1984).

E. Käsemann, "The Beginnings of Christian Theology" and "On the Subject of Primitive Christian Apocalyptic" in *New Testament Questions of Today* (Philadelphia: Fortress, 1969) 82–107, 108–137.

K. Koch, *The Rediscovery of Apocalyptic* (SBT 2d Ser. 22; London: SCM, 1972).

J. L. Martyn, "Apocalyptic Antinomies in Paul's Letter to the Galatians," *NTS* 31 (1985) 410–24.

P. Vielhaur, "Apocalypses and Related Subjects: Introduction: Apocalyptic" in *New Testament Apocrypha,* E. Hennecke, W. Schneemelcher, R. McL. Wilson, eds. (Philadelphia: Westminster, 1965) 2.582–600.

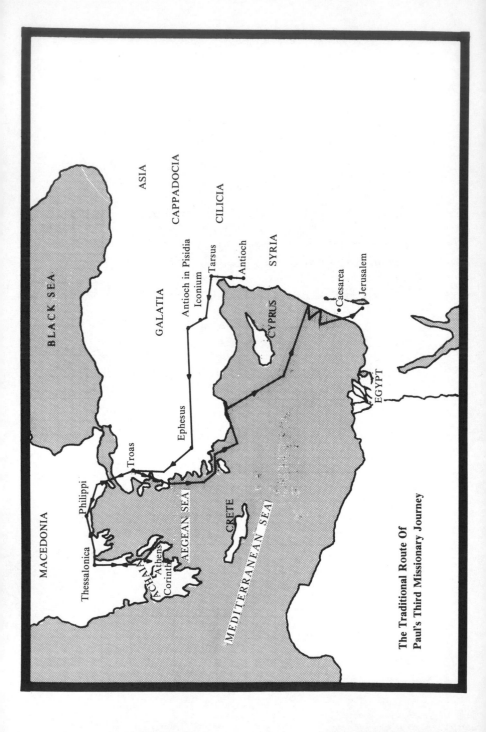

**The Traditional Route Of
Paul's Third Missionary Journey**

Paul the Apostle: Work, Travels, and Letters

Method for Study of the Letters

In the following portion of the book, the method of study applied to the texts is as follows:

Introduction

    I. Paul's Relationship to the Church or Individual
       A. First Contact
       B. After Departure

    II. The Problem That Elicited the Particular Letter

    III. Those Whom Paul Opposes by Means of the Letter (if anyone)

    IV. Theology of the Opponents *or* the Thinking Associated with the Problem

    V. Structure of Paul's Letter—His Response or Debate

    VI. Paul's Solution or Advice

    VII. Theological Key(s) to the Letter

At times it is impossible to study a letter using all the points on this outline—for example, Paul had no contact with the church at Rome before he wrote Romans. Thus this outline for study will be adapted to suit the particular letter under consideration.

The Undisputed Letters

1 Thessalonians

Thessalonica was the capital city of the Roman province Macedonia. Today the modern city Thessaloniki stands in northeastern Greece on the ruins of the ancient site. Thessalonica was prominent not only because it was a provincial capital, but also because it lay on the great Roman military highway Via Egnatia which ran from Byzantium in eastern Europe through Philippi and Thessalonica in Macedonia and on to Rome in the West. In the first century Thessalonica was a large, populous city.

Paul's Relationship to the Thessalonians

After the Jerusalem Conference Paul and Barnabas went back to the church in Antioch, where they remained for some time. A controversy arose in Antioch (compare Gal 2:11-14 and Acts 15:36-40) and subsequently Paul and Barnabas went separate ways. Paul now formed a team with Silvanus (called Silas in Acts). These two worked their way through Syria, Cilicia, Phrygia, and Galatia, making their way northwest across Asia Minor to the Aegean seacoast town of Troas. En route Paul and Silvanus took on Timothy as a missionary associate. From Troas they sailed the northeastern island route to the Macedonian seaport Neapolis. From this port Paul, Silvanus, and Timothy traveled inland on the Via Egnatia to Philippi where they remained for "some days" and won the first of their European converts to Christ (Acts 16:12-15). While in Philippi Paul and Silvanus became involved in an uproar and were incarcerated, but they were subsequently released and asked to leave the city. Then they made their way farther along the Via Egnatia to Thessalonica.

Acts 17:1–10 recounts Paul's brief missionary activity in Thessalonica. Upon entering the capital city Paul and Silvanus (and Timothy?) went to the local synagogue. They used this location as a base for missionary work for about three weeks. The Acts account says Paul argued from scripture that "Jesus . . . is the Christ." Some listeners were persuaded and joined Paul and Silvanus. These believers were obviously Jews, for Acts adds that besides these "a large number of God-fearing Greeks and not a few of the leading women" were persuaded by Paul's preaching. Apparently a house-church was formed at the home of one Jason who turns out to be a Roman citizen. The synagogue Jews who did not believe are described as "being jealous," and thus they solicited the assistance of the local rabble (Acts literally calls these ruffians "some no-account marketplace frequenters"). The combined forces stormed the house of Jason and dragged him and "the rest" (though not including Paul and Silvanus) before the city authorities who levied a fine on the Christians. As a result of this volatile incident the Thessalonian Christians sent Paul and Silvanus away at night to Beroea.

One often reads that Paul's stay at Thessalonica was merely three or four weeks. This is an erroneous conclusion drawn by an unimaginative reading of the text. The only information in Acts concerning the length of Paul's activity in Thessalonica regards the time spent *in the synagogue*. From the statement that Paul remained in the synagogue "three weeks" one cannot decide how long Paul and his companions were in the city, for the period at Jason's house is undefined. Indeed, that the message took and that the converts were devoted, even protective, would imply a period longer than three weeks, though the end of Paul's stay was unforeseen and came not by his choice.

The Acts account continues by telling of Paul's brief stay and successful missionary work in Beroea (17:10–15). This work also came to an abrupt halt when the Thessalonian synagogue Jews followed the missionary band to this town and created another disturbance. Acts 17:14 says Paul alone left town, leaving Silvanus and Timothy behind, but this claim is difficult, if not impossible, to reconcile with Paul's own words in 1 Thess 3:1–5. Paul seems to say that Timothy went with him to Athens and then from Athens he sent Timothy to Thessalonica to survey the situation and to sustain the Thessalonians. In any case Paul traveled to Athens and, working alone, preached there briefly—though not with unusual success (see Acts 17:16–34). From Athens Paul went to Corinth, where he was joined by Silvanus and Timothy who apprised him of the situation among the Thessalonians (1 Thess 3:6). From the church in Thessalonica Timothy brought both his own observations and the congregation's questions. In response Paul writes this entirely friendly letter. There is no evidence of a full-blown crisis. One detects no sign of trouble-making interlopers among the Thessalonians as one does in some of Paul's other letters. Instead the church appears to have been afflicted from without, and this persecution (and perhaps the death of some member[s] of the church) seems to have caused questions, even doubts, to arise within the community.

From the knowledge that Paul arrived in Corinth in late A.D. 50 and that Timothy only recently joined him there, it is likely that Paul wrote to the Thessalonians toward the end of 50, but certainly no later than 51. Thus, scholars regard 1 Thessalonians as the earliest (preserved) Pauline letter. There is no questioning of its authenticity, since its vocabulary, style, and thought patterns cohere with the preponderance of the writings in the Pauline corpus.

The Problem That Elicited This Letter

The situation in Thessalonica may be inferred based upon the remarks of Paul in this letter. According to these, it seems that some "fellow countrymen" of the Thessalonian Christians (perhaps the same old troublemakers) are persecuting the believers. Part of the way these adversaries make the Thessalonians uncomfortable is to cast aspersions on the integrity of the apostle who had left town in the dead of night. If one may read Paul's statements in 1 Thess 2:3–8 as a response to such criticism, then the critics are saying that Paul is an offensive, erroneous, unclean (in terms of the law), greedy trickster who is out for his personal glory. Moreover, this attack on Paul is designed to undermine the Thessalonian's faith in the apostle and thereby in the veracity of his message. What, in fact, Paul's (and his gospel's) critics do is compare him with the run-of-the-mill Cynic street preachers who inhabited the cities of the Hellenistic world. Generally and at worst these were disheveled peripatetic so-called philosophers who upbraided their listeners and then extracted funds from them as a kind of guilt-offering. In the ancient world many were chary of the common lot of Cynics. For example, in a satirical piece, *Philosophies for Sale,* the second century (A.D.) writer Lucian of Samosata has a Cynic advise,

> You should be impudent and bold, and should abuse all and each, both kings and commoners, for thus they will admire you and think you manly. Let your language be barbarous, your voice discordant and just like the barking of a dog . . . put off modesty, decency and moderation and wipe away blushes from your face completely . . . do boldly in full view of all what another would not do in secret . . . you will not need education and doctrine and drivel, but this is a short cut to fame.

In another satire, *The Dead Come to Life,* Lucian recounts the opening of a Cynic's wallet-bag, which should have contained a book or scrolls and simple food stuff like lupines (edible herb seeds) or bread. Instead the bag held "gold, perfume, a razor, a mirror, and a set of dice." Thus Lucian expressed and appealed to the then popular notion (not entirely ill-founded) that most so-called Cynics were hypocrites and freeloaders.

While classical Cynics are long gone, one still encounters their heirs today in the form of self-acclaimed evangelists who severely chide the folly of their listeners and then pass the hat. Now as then these hucksters provide entertainment for the masses, make a few converts of particularly guilt-ridden souls, and manage to extract a living from those who hear them.

Unfortunately, given the pattern of his missionary activity in Thessalonica, it was easy to compare Paul to these people. The Thessalonians had seen such people, and once Paul was no longer among them, such comparisons promoted doubts about both the apostle and his message. When such unfavorable comparisons were made they might wonder whether they had merely been gulled by just another screwball or pettifogger.

In addition, the Thessalonians are themselves under attack. This is clear from 2:13–16 and perhaps 3:3–4, but one cannot discern or even infer the exact nature of the "afflictions" suffered by the Thessalonians.

Those Whom Paul Opposes in 1 Thessalonians

Paul identifies those who afflict the Thessalonian Christians in 2:14 as "your own fellow countrymen." Scholars debate the exact meaning of this designation and offer a variety of interpretations of whom Paul opposes. Wayne A. Meeks is representative of what is perhaps the majority position among critical scholars. He argues that the so-called fellow countrymen are clearly distinguishable from the analogous group of Judean Jews mentioned in 2:14. Thus he judges the Thessalonian Christians and those persecuting them to be Gentiles, not Jews, as one might conclude upon the basis of the Acts account.

Helmut Koester is representative of those who offer another solution by judging 1 Thess 2:13–16 (or 2:14–16) to be a later anti-Jewish interpolation into Paul's original letter. Those who draw this conclusion argue both that vv. 13–16 break the flow of 1 Thess 2 and that the anti-Jewish tone of the lines contradicts Paul's statements in Romans 9–11.

Recent, instructive work by Karl P. Donfried challenges both these interpretations. Following Donfried's lead one can see that 2:13–16 fits well into the flow of 1 Thessalonians. In 2:13 Paul *gives thanks*. He did this in 1:2 (*eucharistein* in Greek) and then in 3:9 he uses the noun *thanksgiving* (*eucharistia*). Moreover, after giving thanks in 1:2 Paul explains one reason for his thankfulness is that the Thessalonians "became imitators" of Paul, Silvanus, Timothy, and even the Lord in receiving affliction (1:6). In the same way after giving thanks in 2:13 Paul explicates that, in part, his thankfulness comes because the Thessalonians "became imitators" of the churches in Judea in receiving affliction from their fellow countrymen. Thus vv. 13–16 do not break the flow of 1 Thess 2; rather they fit into the material in terms of language and logic.

This insight, however, leaves unanswered the objection that the anti-Jewish tone of 2:13–16 contradicts Paul's statements in Romans. In responding to this objection, Donfried gets at the identity of the Thessalonians' "fellow countrymen." He works using a critical method articulated above, namely that Paul's letters are primary source material *and* that the secondary material in Acts may be employed as supplementary information when it does not conflict with Paul's own statements. In Acts 17 those attacking the Christian missionaries and neophytes in Thessalonica are a band of "jealous Jews" and Gentile riffraff, but the Gentiles are merely underlings while the Jews are the real adversaries. If one accepts the reliability of this story—there is nothing in 1 Thessalonians to preclude Jews from being among the recipients of the letter—2:13–16 is not so much an anti-Jewish extrapolation from Thessalonica to Judea as it is a literal parallel recognizing and condemning the activity of Jews in both places who block the progress of the gospel.

But what of the alleged conflict between 2:13–16 and Romans that is cited by those who judge these verses to be an interpolation? Romans 11:25–26 says, "A hardening has come upon part of Israel until the full number of the Gentiles may come in, and thus all of Israel will be saved." 1 Thess 2:16 holds the statement to which some object. The RSV translates, "But God's wrath has come upon them at last (or *completely*, or *forever*)." The problem is this: Will all Israel be saved, as in Romans? Or has God's wrath come upon the hardened part of Israel forever, as in 1 Thessalonians?

To anticipate, there is no conflict! "At last" or "completely" or "forever" poorly translates Paul's words *eis telos,* which literally mean "unto the end." 1 Thess 2:16 should be translated, " 'But wrath has come upon them until the end." Notice that both *wrath* and *the end* are apocalyptic concepts, typical of Paul's thought. With this in mind what Paul means in 1 Thess 2:16 becomes clear. He is saying that the cross, which marks the beginning of the end, produced a crisis that reveals God's judgment, *now*. The jealous Thessalonian Jews are, as Romans says, the hardened part of Israel. And now, in the interim between the cross and the coming of Christ, wrath has come upon them and is upon them to the end. This is as far as 1 Thessalonians goes, but Romans continues the story. From Romans one learns that at the coming of Christ, at the end, the outcome is set—God's mercy will prevail and all Israel will be saved.

By taking Acts seriously, by taking Paul's apocalyptic vision into account, and by reading both 1 Thessalonians and Romans in this light, one makes sense of 2:13–16. One comes to see who the opponents in Thessalonica were and to understand the situation Paul is addressing in his letter to the Christians there. For example, one may understand that the persecutors were diaspora Jews who were law-observant and who, therefore, found Paul's message offensive in that it was law-free.

Moreover, Paul's success with the God-fearers would irritate these Jews, for they had worked themselves to bring the Gentiles into the synagogue and hoped the God-fearers would become full proselytes to Judaism. With this background in mind the letter becomes more easily intelligible.

The Structure of Paul's Letter

The letter is somewhat unusual in form. The note sounded in the *thanksgiving* (1:2–10) resounds even through chapter three. One hears the tone of the *parenesis* (5:12–22) as early as chapter four. For such reasons one who consults scholarly commentaries in studying 1 Thessalonians encounters a remarkable variety of descriptions of the structure of the letter. What follows is one analysis of the letter's form; others are certainly possible.

1 THESSALONIANS	
Salutation	1:1
Thanksgiving	1:2–10
Body of the Letter	2:1–5:11
Parenesis	5:12–22
Closing	5:23–28

Salutation. The letter names Paul, Silvanus, and Timothy as its authors. The three claim no titles and name no role they play in the life of early Christianity. Such brevity is unusual in Paul's letters, for Paul usually says he is a servant, apostle, or prisoner of Jesus Christ.

In addressing the Thessalonians, Paul reminds them that they are a congregation *in* God and Christ (*ekklesia* in Greek, usually translated "church," also means "congregation"). Thus, these people are already in the realm of the saving power of God. Therefore, Paul can greet them with his Christian salutation, "grace and peace."

Thanksgiving. Paul begins to praise the Thessalonians here (1:2–

10) and continues to do so throughout the letter (see 2:20; 3:7–9; 4:9). He recalls the calling of the Thessalonians, surely stirring memories of a sacred moment for the readers.

The Body of the Letter. Because Paul gives thanks and continues his praise of the Thessalonians, it is difficult to decide exactly where the body of the letter begins. That he turns back to himself and his colleagues and their former work among the Thessalonians at 2:1 probably signals the commencement of the body, however. When Paul rehearses his own time among the readers (2:1–12) he carefully selects images that distance him from the typical Cynic street preacher: he had no philosopher's cloak (2:5), he was gentle as a nurse (2:7), and he exhorted them like a father with his children (2:11). Moreover he reminds the Thessalonians that he worked night and day, supporting himself, so that he was not financially dependent upon the Thessalonian Christians as he proclaimed the gospel among them.

In 2:13–20 Paul reminds the Thessalonians again, more elaborately, of their own conversion. Here he interprets their experience of persecution as being in accordance with the pattern of those in whom and among whom God is at work, namely Jesus Christ, the churches in Judea, and himself. In vv. 17–20 Paul casts the experience of persecution in cosmic, apocalyptic terms, naming Satan as the force behind worldly persecution of those in God's camp.

Chapter three explains the writing of the letter. Paul tells of his sending Timothy from Athens back to Thessalonica to facilitate the faithfulness of the Thessalonians. Paul tells how he rejoiced at the good news Timothy brought when he rejoined Paul. Finally Paul prays to come again to Thessalonica. Obviously he is not going immediately, so he writes to the church instead.

At 4:1 Paul turns to a series of exhortations. These are not simple parenesis but broader teachings. One might suspect this material is the sort of information Paul usually delivered in person, but since he had left Thessalonica suddenly and had been prevented from returning, he sends the information in written form. Briefly, Paul instructs the Thessalonians on a decent lifestyle (4:1–8), Christian love (4:9–12), and death and Christian assurance (4:13–18). Having raised the issue of Christ's coming as the basis for Christian hope, Paul moves to deny there are discernible signs for fathoming *when* the coming will be.

Paul tells the readers that they are afforded no knowledge of *when*, only *how*. Christ will come suddenly and unexpectedly, like a thief in the night. Knowing this provides Christians with motivation for everyday living—expecting Christ and knowing they are not experiencing, nor will they experience, the wrath of God. Remarkably at 4:18 and 5:11 in concluding his eschatological teachings, Paul instructs the Thessalonians to use this information to comfort, encourage, and build up one another! In other words, knowing of Christ's coming gives the Thessalonian Christians hope and frees them to care for others.

Parenesis. Verses 12–22 of chapter five are a pointed series of brief instructions that include directions for the treatment of both Christian leaders and the less than exemplary members of the congregation (5:12–15). Verses 16–22 are eight imperative remarks. First, there are three positive statements (rejoice; pray; and give thanks), commanding activities that are said to be the will of God. Then one finds two prohibitions (do not quench the Spirit; do not despise prophecy). Rather than doing what Paul forbids, the Thessalonians are told in three final positive commands what they should do (test everything; hold on to what is good; avoid every sort of evil). Apparently Paul believed doing these things prevents quenching the Spirit and despising prophecy.

Closing. This part of the letter is expanded from the usual Hellenistic form. Then the closing begins with a full benediction based on *peace*. The Thessalonians are directed to pray for the apostle and his companions and to greet one another with a "holy kiss." (Ancients greeted one another with a kiss as moderns do with a handshake. The kiss was made holy by being given in the realm of God.) Next Paul instructs the Thessalonians to read the letter to everyone, and then he concludes with a benediction of *grace*. The movement from *peace* to *grace* in the benediction reverses the order of the opening of the letter and brings the communication full circle to its end.

Paul's Advice to the Thessalonians

Paul is straightforward with his advice. He reminds the Thessalonians that they were delivered from wrath by Jesus Christ (1:10) and are, therefore, in the realm of the saving power of God (1:1; 5:23). Therein, although they are experiencing persecution, they are secure and need only to stand fast in the Lord (3:8). They can do this by following the instructions issued in the eight imperatives in Paul's parenesis (5:16–22). Paul tells the readers they have a solid Christian history and need only to keep on living more and more as they have (4:1).

Theological Keys to 1 Thessalonians

This letter is a striking example of how Paul used his apocalyptic vision of the triumph of God to assure and instruct those among whom he labored. In the midst of persecution the word of gracious comfort the apostle extends to those in distress is the provocative reminder that they have been rescued from wrath by Jesus Christ who was raised from the dead and who will come from heaven. The pie is not merely in the sky, however, for already God's final judgment is evident. On the one hand people are being saved and on the other those doing Satan's work are experiencing God's wrath.

Paul gives his readers details about the coming of Christ. But this is not merely information about the future, the possession of which guarantees one salvation. Strikingly, *Paul uses eschatology as the basis for hope that determines the nature of daily life*. In other words, Christian eschatology and everyday life are bonded—the former determining the latter.

BIBLIOGRAPHY

E. Best, *A Commentary on the First and Second Epistles to the Thessalonians* (BNTC; London: Black, 1972).

J. C. Hurd, "Thessalonians, First Letter to the," *IDBSup* 900.

K. P. Donfried, "Paul and Judaism: 1 Thessalonians 2:13–16 as a Test Case," *Int* 38 (1984) 242–53.

A. J. Malherbe, "Gentle as a Nurse," *NovT* 12 (1970) 203–17.

Galatians

In the strictest sense Galatia was a territory in northern Asia Minor. Originally the region was populated by Celts who migrated there from Gaul in the first half of the third century B.C. (In Greek, *galatai* [Galatians] is a variant of *keltai* [Celts].) In 25 B.C. the last of the Galatian kings died, leaving his kingdom in the hands of the Romans, who reorganized the area into a province by adding other districts (Isauria, parts of Lycaonia, Paphlagonia, Pisidia, Phrygia, and Pontus) to Galatia. But the province as a whole bore no official name; rather, it went by the names of its parts.

This ambiguous situation motivates debate among scholars who query whether Paul's letter to the Galatian congregations is addressed to (a) churches throughout the larger Roman province, especially the southern portion, or (b) churches in the territory proper, i.e., the northern portion. This issue is often referred to as the North Galatia/South Galatia Debate, though a more accurate description of the question is the Galatian Territorial/Provincial Debate. The importance of the problem is this: the ethnic make-up of the population of the territory and that of the remainder of the province were distinct. In the north lay Ancyra, the capital of the province, whereas in the south, in the districts of Lycaonia and Phrygia, lay Pisidia Antioch, Iconium, Lystra, and Derbe. Ancyra was a large important trade center with a cosmopolitan population surrounding it as was typical of Roman provincial capital cities; but the southern towns were smaller, unimportant— they have been called "quiet backwaters." Nevertheless, if Paul is addressing the citizens of the southern portion of the province, one has more extensive information in Acts to assist in understanding who the recipients were and, thereby, to interpret the letter per se.

As observed above, Paul's custom was to settle in a provincial capital city and from an established base to evangelize the region by sending his associates out to found satellite congregations. From knowledge of this habit alone, one might speculate that Ancyra and the northern territory are the more likely candidates for a Pauline mission, but from Gal 4:13 it appears Paul's work among the Galatians was unplanned and came about because of an illness; so a deviation from Paul's normal pattern of evangelization is possible. Yet, other facts support the interpretation of "Galatia" as a reference to the northern territory. For example, the name Galatia occurs in ancient inscriptions only for the territory. Moreover, the citizens of the larger province—outside the territory proper—though associated with Galatia politically, did not regard or refer to themselves as Galatians.

Paul's Relationship to the Galatians

After identifying the Galatians as the citizens of the northern territory, one turns to Acts 16:6; 18:23, and Gal 4:12–15 for information about Paul's first contact with those to whom this letter is addressed. The reference in Acts 16 is a pure telescoping of time, and one learns merely that Paul went through the area. Paul himself writes of his original dealings with the Galatians, saying, "You know it was because of an illness of the flesh that I preached the gospel to you at first." He continues, "You would have plucked out your eyes and given them to me—if possible." These lines and the mention of the "large letters" of Paul's handwriting (6:11) lead some interpreters to conclude that Paul had problems with his vision and this forced him to reside among the Galatians. Perhaps this is true, though one cannot say with certainty. Nevertheless, the reader of Galatians may infer that Paul's first contact with the Galatians was in a time of personal crisis.

From Acts 16–19 (to retrace Paul's travels briefly) one learns that Paul first made his way to Galatia shortly after the Jerusalem Conference (see Acts 15). From Galatia, Paul moved west, crossing Asia Minor and then sailing across the Aegean Sea to the Roman province of Macedonia where he founded several congregations. He traveled south into Greece, eventually settling in Corinth for a year and a half. From Corinth Paul sailed back to Asia Minor, now to the port of Ephesus. He continued south as far as Caesarea and then headed north to Antioch. From Antioch Paul continued north through Asia Minor into and throughout Galatia and Phrygia. (Perhaps this second visit is the reason Paul writes in Gal 4:13 of when he "at first" preached the gospel to the Galatians.) Eventually, Paul returned to Ephesus, where he remained for two years and three months (see Acts 19:1–20), from the fall of A.D. 52 until the spring of A.D. 55.

Acts tells remarkably little about so long a stay, but it was probably here, in Ephesus, that Paul penned his letters to the church at Corinth and the churches in Galatia. From his references in these letters to the "collection," one can schematize the chronology of Paul's writings from Ephesus. Galatians seems to be the earliest letter, for in 2:10 Paul merely mentions the collection. In 1 Corinthians he plans it in earnest, and in 2 Corinthians one sees that the project is well under way. Thus, this letter was most likely written early in the Ephesian residence.

The Problem That Elicited This Letter

According to Gal 1:6, Paul wrote to the Galatians because they were deserting their calling by his preaching and turning to what he caustically calls a "different gospel." This other gospel was proclaimed among the Galatians by a group of outsiders who came among them after Paul's departure and who were probably in their midst when Paul wrote. Paul says the Galatians are "foolish . . . bewitched" (3:1). They have moved from their Christian origin in the Spirit to the realm of the flesh. Indeed, Paul suggests that the Galatians were seeking to receive the Spirit out of *the workings of the law* rather than out of *the hearing of faith*. In other words, under the influence of those who have come among them, the Galatians were moving toward law-observance. This is clear from the references in 4:10 to the calendar, in 5:2 to circumcision, and in 5:3 to the "whole law."

Those Whom Paul Opposes in Galatians

In order to understand what Paul is saying in Galatians, it is necessary to gain some idea of who the outsiders who have come among the Galatians are and what they have said that has caused the problem. To do this one must engage in a "mirror-reading" of the text, i.e., the problem in Galatia and those whom Paul opposes must be reconstructed from Paul's descriptions and statements in the letter itself.

This is somewhat similar to listening to someone talking on the telephone. From what is said on one end of the line, an attentive listener may be able to infer what was said by the other partner in the conversation. This involves speculation, so there are risks that the "other" side of the conversation may be misunderstood or distorted; but without this reconstruction, Paul's statements are completely incomprehensible. Thus, one must run the risks of reconstruction, but only with extreme caution.

Paul records three relatively neutral pieces of information about those who came among the Galatians after his departure. Of them he says:

1. They preach "another gospel," different from that preached in Galatia by Paul; he says it is a perversion of the gospel (1:6–7). This is Paul's description, however; and an unbiased reader of the letter should infer that in the minds of these preachers, the gospel they proclaim is *the* gospel, not a perversion.

2. They "trouble" the Galatians (1:7). The message of these preachers disturbs or frightens the Galatians; it "unsettles" them (5:12).

3. The preachers in Galatia are themselves circumcised (6:13).

These statements serve as fixed points in the effort to conceptualize those whom Paul opposed in Galatia. Using other information in the letter, one may draw between the points to develop a fuller picture. Doing so, it seems that after Paul departed from Galatia some evangelists came there independently preaching a message—enough like Paul's to be regarded as "the gospel," but sufficiently different for Paul to call it a perversion or "another gospel." This new preaching has stirred up the Galatians. Paul seems to associate these people with the "false brethren" of the Jerusalem Conference (2:4). This inference makes sense, for the preachers clearly advocate observance of the law by Christians. Moreover, in addition to preaching a gospel different from that proclaimed by Paul, Gal 1:10 suggests that these evangelists have accused Paul of being a *people-pleaser*, a preacher of a watered-down gospel.

In fairness to these evangelists, they probably understood themselves to be Christian Jews engaged in a law-observant mission to the Gentiles, not primarily Paul's opponents. They do appear to have criticized Paul for preaching a law-free gospel, but it is the apostle who cast them into the role of adversaries, not they. Thus, the major task at this point is to discern what these people considered the "good news" to be.

The Theology of the Opponents and the Thinking Associated with the Problem

From Paul's letter, one learns something of the content of the Galatian preachers' proclamation:

1. The law is their point of departure and the heart of their theology (5:1–4). They probably speak of "the law of Christ" (6:2)—for this is not a Pauline phrase. They probably teach that God's law was affirmed and interpreted by God's Messiah, so that Jesus is the Messiah of the law. Their theology has *an additive pattern*: they view the law as primary and *add* Christ to it as the authoritative interpreter. They probably teach that to obey the law as interpreted by Christ is to become "Abraham's offspring" (3:6–18).

2. The "good news" is *news* and *good* for the Gentiles. This is obvious since the preachers are in Galatia, advocating the law among Gentiles. The law, formerly given to Israel alone, is now available to Gentiles through the interpretation of the Messiah. The preachers themselves are probably not meticulous in their observance of the law (6:13). They appear to understand the law, as they say it is interpreted by the Messiah, to be a reduction of the former, more stringent requirements. They focus on the overt portions of the law (circumcision and calendar) so that the law is now for all. Moreover, they do not see the problem Paul recognizes, namely, the conflict between Christ and the law. Instead, they think of law-observance as an obligatory sign, as the very manageable human end of a bargain with God.

3. Clearly the preachers in Galatia used the Old Testament as a textual tool in dissemination of their religious propaganda. They probably understood the Old Testament as ritual prescription and believed and taught that proper observance of the prescription assured one of receiving the Spirit (see 3:2–3). Throughout Galatians one sees Paul take up certain of their favorite texts and engage himself in rather original exegesis. What is remarkable is that Paul and the preachers *agree* that proper interpretation of the Old Testament provides truth and is essential.

4. The "good news" proclaimed by the preachers was conditional.

At 4:17 Paul employs the image of the gate and gatekeepers. The preachers at Galatia have threatened to shut the Galatians out if they failed to comply with the admonition to law-observance. The preachers must have understood the law as the narrow gate to salvation and themselves as the gatekeepers who guarded the way of righteousness.

5. The preachers appear to have taught that the "key" to the gate was law-observance (4:17), especially circumcision (5:2, 13).

The Structure of Paul's Letter

GALATIANS	
Salutation	1:1–5
Thanksgiving	none
Body of the Letter	1:6–5:12
Parenesis	5:13–6:10
Closing	6:11–18

Salutation. Paul begins the letter in his typical fashion with a salutation. Notice that Paul alone addresses the Galatians; he names no colleague in the opening, though as almost an afterthought he mentions the band of his missionary associates. Moreover, Paul's self-designation has an apologetic ring, for he identifies himself from the outset with the *power of God*. The greeting in v. 3 with the mention of "grace and peace" is a stock Pauline formula, but vv. 4–5 expand the greeting significantly. In these verses Paul makes clear that Christ's saving activity transpired in order to deliver humanity from "the present evil age." These verses are a prolepsis of the teaching in 3:13 that Christ himself became cursed to deliver humanity from "the curse of the law."

Thanksgiving. Galatians is an anomaly among the Pauline letters in that it is the only letter that does *not* include a thanksgiving. With regard to the situation in Galatia Paul probably had nothing for which to be thankful.

The Body of the Letter. The heart of the letter falls into two broad sections. Gal 1:6–2:21 is Paul's personal defense of his apostleship. He offers this section in response to an apparent attack by the preachers in Galatia on himself and his office. He focuses on the divine nature of both his calling and the origin of "his" gospel. The degree of Paul's agitation is discernible in the extreme lengths to which he makes his protest. This section contains invaluable information about Paul's life and his self-understanding.

In 3:1–5:12 Paul offers arguments and exegetical demonstrations concerning the freedom of the Christian from the law. The section may appear to be a rambling series of remarks, but there is a logic behind the arrangement of the material. It would be misleading to suggest that the pattern of the argument is a polished rhetorical device, for scrutiny of this section does not reveal sufficient balance. Yet, there is a deliberateness to Paul's thought.

He begins with the Galatians' own original experience of salvation. He continues with a rabbinic-style midrashic interpretation of the story of Abraham, making the point that Abraham was saved by faith, not by the workings of the law. In the central portion of this section Paul boldly contrasts Christ and the law. As Abraham was saved by faith in the promise of God, so the Christian is saved by faith in the fulfillment of that promise, namely by faith in Jesus Christ. Neither Abraham nor the Christian is saved by the workings of the law, for the workings of the law are incapable of saving anyone, ever (3:21). Toward the end of this section Paul takes up the Sarah/Hagar story, a corollary to the Abraham material. This he treats in the allegorical interpretative style of popular Hellenistic philosophy (4:24). From this Old Testament argument Paul returns to the Galatians and concludes the section by directly admonishing the Galatians to avoid all trappings of the law.

In addition to the bold strokes of the arguments, Paul shows his disdain for the preachers by portraying them as real nobodies (5:10) and by sending them a crude wish (5:12). The earthy dimension of the apostle's personality comes out in these lines, but the translations make him appear considerably tamer than he was. For example, RSV renders 5:12, "I wish those who unsettle you would mutilate themselves!"—a strong statement. And a bit more fire is present in the JB, "Tell those who are disturbing you I would like to see the knife slip."

But a literal translation of the apostle's statement reads, "I really wish that the ones who are confusing you (concerning circumcision) would lop it off!"

Parenesis. Paul issues ethical instructions in 5:13–6:10. He calls for the Galatians to preserve their freedom by obeying the Spirit, and then he gives them concrete directions. In this section Paul offers the well-known list of the fruit of the Spirit. Without examining the catalogue in detail, one should notice that in 5:22 Paul includes *faith* (*pistis* in Greek, some translations unwisely render this as "faithfulness") as a fruit of the Spirit. Remarkably, the apostle is saying that *faith itself* is a product of God's Spirit, not something that humans generate. It is not the case that God has acted in Christ, and now, if humans respond to that act with faith, they are saved. Rather, Paul says that part of what God has done in Jesus Christ is to create saving faith in human beings.

Closing. Paul concludes his letter in 6:11–18. He begins an extended statement in 6:11 that peaks in 6:15, "Neither circumcision counts for anything, nor uncircumcision, but a new creation!" Verses 16–18 pronounce a benediction. Embedded in this final "good word" is a peculiar disjoining of the apostle from the Galatian turmoil (6:17), and though it has the ring of a hex, it is a wish that unfortunately never came true, for time and again the apostle encountered troubles from those who opposed him. (Although there is no way to prove it, I like to think that the very preservation of Paul's letter to the Galatians means that the congregations read it, were persuaded by it, and preserved it for subsequent guidance.)

Paul's Advice to the Galatians

Paul insists that the gospel he preached among the Galatians is the only gospel. Anything else, no matter what it is called or who preaches it, is a perversion. Paul states boldly that his apostolic commission and the origin of his message were the results of divine revelation. He did not learn his message from any human. In contrast, he suggests that the preachers in Galatia are concerned only with "the flesh." This is seen in their focus on keeping the law, especially in their concern with circumcision. They are bound up with human achievement in the present evil age, *not* with the Spirit which is known and experienced by the power of God the same power that raised Jesus from the dead.

One of the main lines of Paul's argument in Galatians is his juxtaposition of faith and the law. This contrast reflects Paul's apocalyptic mind-set, for he thinks of faith and the law as elements in two opposing realms, one potent and the other impotent (3:21). One sees this at 2:16 where Paul speaks of "the faith of Christ" and "the workings of the law." Literally, his phrases in Greek say, "out of the faith of Christ and out of the workings of the law." He thinks here of two realms "out of" which powerful results emanate.

For Paul these words (along with others like Spirit and flesh) function as technical terms that describe two opposing *realms*, one God's and the other in opposition to God. They are cosmic in scope, and humans are in either one realm or the other. Persons in God's realm are being saved, whereas those in the other realm are lost, cursed. Accordingly, those "in faith" are saved and those "under the law" are cursed, for Jesus Christ rescued those "in faith" whereas those "under the law" are caught up in the law's impotence and are trapped.

The good news for those under the law is that Jesus Christ gave himself, invading the realm of the law and becoming cursed as he died crucified. And then God revealed his power, overcame the curse, and saved humanity by raising Jesus from the dead. Moreover, from "the faith of Christ" comes *faith itself* (5:22), by which humans, like Abraham, are set right with God. Contrary to the claim of the preachers in Galatia, salvation is not tied to human achievement (the workings of the law). For saving faith is not a human achievement; it is a fruit of the Spirit (5:22), a gracious gift from God. In contrast, from "the workings of the law," the system of righteousness advocated by the preachers, comes "the curse of the law" (3:13) whereby all things are "consigned to/under sin" (3:22).

Paul says that the preachers proclaim "the workings of the law"— a new covenant of the law as they say it has been renewed through Christ. Against this Paul proclaims that with Christ the law came to an end, and so there is no more law and no more circumcision as a sign of the covenant. Paul takes Abraham as an example in an original piece of Old Testament interpretation (surely it never occurred to anyone to interpret the Abraham story as one finds it in Galatians before

Paul did so). He says that God made a promise to Abraham before the law existed. Jesus Christ is the fulfillment of God's promise to Abraham. Thus, when one compares Christ and the law, Christ has chronological priority and theological superiority over the law, for the promise preceded the law and Christ fulfills the promise.

At 3:15–18 Paul shows the ridiculousness of the additive pattern (Law + Christ = new law) advocated by the preachers in Galatia. He says that attempts to add Christ to the law show ignorance of the priority of God's promise to Abraham. One cannot add Christ to the law because the promise and its fulfillment stand above the law and coexist apart from the existence of the law.

God's Promise .... The Fulfillment of
to   the Promise
Abraham   (The Law)   in Christ

Moreover, Paul reminds the Galatians (and the preachers?) that the promise was to Abraham's offspring (singular), namely Jesus Christ, not to Abraham's offspring (plural), namely the law-observant and Christ. Above all, however, Christ was cursed by the law because he was crucified (3:13); so there is no way simply to harmonize him, as the preachers in Galatia do, with the very law that cursed him.

Theological Keys to Galatians

Paul perceives that salvation comes through the power of God: Paul was called by this power, Jesus Christ was raised by it, and the Galatians have faith because of God's power.

From this starting point Paul sees that the Galatians have made a heinous mistake in turning to the law, for humans are cursed by the workings of the law. Since salvation is based in God's promise to Abraham and the fulfillment of the promise in Jesus Christ, the law has nothing to do with the promise—indeed, the law came from angels, not from God himself (3:19–20). Paul understands that the law is not against or contrary to the promise, but it has nothing to do with it (3:21). The angels gave the law as a statement of the will of God, meant for the good of humanity, but humans misunderstood the law. They thought it provided a means of salvation through their obedience to it. But Paul says the law is impotent and those humans caught up with the workings of the law are trapped in its impotence and, thereby, cursed.

In Christ, the fulfillment of the promise, God acted to save humanity from its involvement with the impotent, "elemental spirits of the universe," one of which was the law. Christ himself became cursed by the law, for according to the law his death by crucifixion made him accursed by God (3:13 and see Deut 21:23). Nevertheless, God raised Jesus from the dead and thereby demonstrated his power, that Jesus Christ is his Son, and that the law is impotent.

Paul's message to the Galatians is that involvement with the law is enslavement to the flesh. He calls for the Galatians to abandon the error of their ways and to stand fast "in Christ" (not "under the law"), for Jesus Christ, and he alone, means freedom (5:1).

BIBLIOGRAPHY

H. D. Betz, *Galatians* (Hermeneia; Philadelphia: Fortress, 1979).

F. F. Bruce, *The Epistle to the Galatians* (NIGTC; Grand Rapids: Eerdmans, 1982).

E. D. Burton, *A Critical and Exegetical Commentary on the Epistle to the Galatians* (ICC; Edinburgh: Clark, 1920).

J. B. Lightfoot, *St. Paul's Epistle to the Galatians* (London: Macmillan, 1865—reprinted by Hendrickson Publishers, 1981).

J. L. Martyn, "A Law-Observant Mission to the Gentiles: The Background of Galatians," *Michigan Quarterly Review* 22 (1983) 221–36.

Idem, Galatians (AB 33A; Garden City: Doubleday, forthcoming).

The Corinthian Correspondence

Among the letters of Paul in the New Testament two are addressed to the church in Corinth. From these letters one learns that Paul wrote more than two letters to that congregation. 1 Cor 5:9 mentions a previous letter, so that canonical 1 Corinthians is at least the second letter from Paul to Corinth. Moreover, in another context Paul writes in 2 Cor 2:3–4 and 7:8 of still another letter—it clearly is not the one called 1 Corinthians in the New Testament. While we will never know exactly how many letters Paul penned to the church in Corinth, from study of 1 and 2 Corinthians scholars estimate that Paul wrote no fewer than four and perhaps as many as seven letters to the Corinthians— with the recognition that any number of other unmentioned letters are possible. We will have more than one occasion below to take up the *lost* letters of Paul, especially in considering 2 Corinthians.

1 Corinthians

The Corinth Paul knew was a thriving new city. The Romans had destroyed the rich, old Corinth in 146 B.C. and it had remained in ruins until Julius Caesar rebuilt it, refounding it as a Roman colony in 44 B.C. and populating the *new* Corinth with Italian freedmen. Others who were game for profit and adventure joined the Italians as Roman Corinth became a cosmopolitan boom town. The city prospered and was at peace, and from 29 B.C. onward Corinth was the seat of the Roman proconsul and the capital of the senatorial province Achaia.

Corinth lay on the narrow isthmus that connects the Greek mainland with the Peloponnesian peninsula. Thus it bordered on two seas—on the east, the Saronic Gulf of the Aegean Sea; on the west, the Corinthian Gulf of the Adriatic Sea. In antiquity the city afforded its residents perhaps twice the excitement of normally colorful seaports, having a legendary penchant toward vice. The first century population was genuinely pluralistic and among the city's inhabitants religious syncretism flourished.

Today a visitor to Corinth finds the former glory in ruins. Only a sleepy little town now exists beside the remains of the ancient splendor.

Paul's Relation to the Corinthians

From Acts 17 and 18 we have traced Paul's travels after he came to Europe from Asia Minor—first in Macedonia (Philippi, Thessalonica, Beroea) and then south to Achaia (Athens) where he eventually resided for a year and a half (Corinth). One learns (from Acts 18) that in Corinth, as was his custom, Paul went to the Jewish section of the city where he met some Jews, apparently Jewish Christians, named Prisca (the Priscilla of Acts) and Aquila. They had been banished from Rome by an edict of Emperor Claudius. They too were tentmakers; and so, with both religion and business in common, Paul stayed with this couple in Corinth.

Paul engaged in missionary activity using the synagogue for a base as long as was possible. Finally, being reviled and opposed, he moved next door to the synagogue to the home of a God-fearer, Titius Justus. The level of success Paul had in the synagogue is clear from the group that Acts says became believers—Crispus, the synagogue president, his household, and many other Jews and Greeks who heard Paul, believed, and were baptized.

After eighteen months the synagogue Jews began a unified attack against Paul. They brought him before the Roman proconsul, Gallio, who showed no interest in the matter and threw it out of court. The Jews grabbed their new synagogue president, Sosthenes, and beat him before the proconsul's tribunal, but Gallio continued to ignore them.

The Acts account continues, saying that "after many days longer" Paul left Corinth. The reader is not told why, but given the known dislike of Roman officials for disorder in their jurisdictions, one might not go wrong by speculating that Paul was encouraged to depart from Corinth in a more official fashion than is reported in Acts. Whatever the circumstances of Paul's leaving, he sailed east from Corinth and went to Ephesus. Acts records that after a brief stay in this city Paul sailed southeast to Caesarea. From there he traveled on land to Antioch where he remained for "some time," and then he passed through Asia Minor, especially Galatia and Phrygia, on his way back to Ephesus. Paul resided in Ephesus for two years and three months. The length of the stay and certain remarks made in his letters lead some scholars to conclude that Paul must have been imprisoned in Ephesus for at least part of the time. There is, however, no concrete evidence to confirm this theory. Nevertheless, it was in Ephesus that Paul engaged in a series of communications with the church in Corinth. One ascertains this from 1 Corinthians itself, for Paul mentions a previous letter to the Corinthians in 1 Cor 5:9 and discloses his whereabouts in 1 Cor 16:8.

At the time of the writing of 1 Corinthians Paul must have been in Ephesus for some time, for at 1 Cor 16:5–9 he shows he is making plans to leave Ephesus. He intends to bring to completion the collection from the non-Palestinian churches for "the poor" in Jerusalem. He says that upon leaving Ephesus he will go first through Macedonia and then through Achaia to Corinth where he may spend some time, perhaps even the winter, before sailing to Judea.

The Problem(s) That Elicited This Letter

The motivation for Paul's writing of 1 Corinthians was tripartite. First, an oral report from Chloe's people (i.e., Christian members of the household of Chloe, who may or may not have been a Christian) informed Paul about the situation in Corinth (1 Cor 1:11). Second, a letter from the church at Corinth to Paul arrived, carried by a delegation, and Paul responds to issues raised in the letter (1 Cor 7:1). Third, Paul apparently talked with the members of the letter delegation, thereby getting additional information (1 Cor 16:17).

From Chloe's people Paul says he has learned of factions or parties that have been formed among the Corinthians. The members of these factions seem to think they maintain a special relation to the one who baptized them, an apostle (Paul, Apollos, Cephas), or even to the one in whose name they were baptized, Christ. They associate their baptism and their lineage through the authoritative figure whom they identify with a commodity that they value highly, namely *wisdom*. Here Paul has been criticized unfavorably as not being wise enough.

From the letter delegation Paul has learned two things (5:1). One problem is that his earlier letter to the Corinthians has been badly misunderstood. He chastised immoral members of the Corinthian church in that letter, but some members of the church took Paul's instructions to mean they should avoid those (immoral persons only?) outside the church. Paul corrects this misperception, saying the Corinthians cannot leave the world. The second problem of which Paul learned from the delegation concerns "the spiritual people" at Corinth. These are members of the congregation who assert their spiritual superiority and demonstrate it in a variety of ways. Paul quotes the slogans of these people in 1 Cor 6:12–13 and 10:23. In fine, they say, "All things are lawful for me." They show their freedom by engaging in incest (5:1), by boasting of immorality (5:2, 6), by suing one another in pagan courts (6:1–8), by patronizing brothels (6:9–20, esp. v. 15), and/or by practicing asceticism (7:1–8:13).

From the Corinthians' letter Paul learns of specific concerns that are related to the foregoing problems. The inquiries of the letter are discernible from Paul's repeated references to the letter, detectable in Paul's phrase, "now concerning" this-or-that (see 7:1, 25; 8:1; 12:1; and 16:1). The list of things about which the Corinthians query the apostle includes: sex and marriage, food offered to pagan gods prior to sale in the market, the gifts of the Spirit, and the collection for the poor in Jerusalem.

Those Whom Paul Opposes in 1 Corinthians

At the time of Paul's writing of 1 Corinthians no outsider agents are evident in the church. Both the baptism parties and the spiritual people are internal problems, and the questions from the congregation have arisen in the course of daily life. Scholars understand the relation, if any, among the baptism parties, the spiritual people, and the questions in the Corinthians' letter in various ways. In the following study the simplest solution is preferred. Briefly stated it is this: Since Paul does not deal with the groups separately, but integrates his directions to them with his answers to the Corinthians' questions, one should understand him to be speaking monolithically. In other words, because Paul directs his attack toward one front, one should assume that the baptism parties, the spiritual people, and the questions are directly related and are facets of the same general problem. This solution will not lead one far astray.

Apparently some Corinthian Christians have brought portions of their past, pagan religious beliefs into their Christian life. Indeed, the pagan past imported into the Corinthians' new religious context in the church (a setting characterized by Paul's proclamation of Christian freedom) has generated serious misunderstandings—like not grasping the meaning of Paul's earlier letter. Apparently, the spiritual people in Corinth have cast the Christian missionaries who worked among them in the role of *mystagogues*, teachers of esoteric wisdom. Thus baptism has become a mystery rite, imparting wisdom. Moreover, the wisdom one receives at baptism is no better than the wisdom of the one who did the baptizing (or of the one in whose name one was baptized), so there was rivalry among the baptismal parties. Furthermore, in this scheme the Lord's Supper is understood as a mystery meal or cultic banquet, and the celebration has broken into the factions that typify some of the Corinthians' (mis-)understanding of Christianity (1 Cor 11:18–19).

Generally, there has been an elevation of "human wisdom" in Corinth—this is Paul's description, not that of the Corinthians. This wisdom, so valued by the spiritual people, is not logic or sound judgment, but a searching for deeper meanings and a yearning for unseen things. It is a lust for special knowledge that sets one above the masses. The clearest examples of this kind of thinking appear in the Gnostic heresies of later Christianity. One group of Gnostics understood that at Jesus' baptism the heavenly Christ had descended upon the human Jesus, but Christ subsequently abandoned Jesus at (or prior to) the cross. Though Gnosticism shows up in a concrete form decades after Paul wrote to the Corinthians, this kind of thought may help explain how in Paul's day certain Corinthians were saying, "To hell with Jesus" (the Greek of 12:3, *anathema Iēsous*, put politely, means "Jesus be cursed [to the infernal regions]"—any good Greek would get the rude point). Clearly the Corinthians were not full-blown Gnostics, but they show signs of nascent gnosticism.

The spiritual people allowed their lifestyles to document their superior, spiritual self-consciousness. This occurred in two ways. Some Corinthians were flagrantly licentious; others were rigidly ascetic. *Both groups*, however, used their morality (loose or stringent) as the basis for boasting. Strikingly, Paul denies the validity of both moral tendencies, but *he roundly denounces the practicing of boasting*.

The Structure of Paul's Letter

There is a kind of progression to Paul's argumentation in 1 Corinthians, for he deals first with the report of Chloe's people, then with the misunderstanding of the earlier letter, and finally with the spiritual people and the problems they generate. Yet, the letter has no real consecutive development of ideas; rather Paul seems to be responding to the reports he received. Moreover, scholars point to Paul's striking interruption of connected themes with excursuses—see 2:6–16; 6:1–

11; 9:1–27; 10:1–13; and 13:1–13—throughout the letter. One gets the impression that the apostle was agitated while writing to Corinth.

1 CORINTHIANS	
Salutation	1:1–3
Thanksgiving	1:4–9
Body of the Letter	1:10–15:52
Parenesis	16:1–18
Closing	16:19–24

Salutation. The letter opens by naming Paul and Sosthenes as co-authors. This Sosthenes is very likely the same Sosthenes mentioned in Acts 18:17. If so, he had once been the president of the synagogue, indeed the one who brought Paul before Gallio's tribunal. Paul describes himself as "called by the will of God to be an apostle." In addressing the Corinthians Paul makes clear that he is in a position to say what God's will is—a claim he makes explicitly in 1 Cor 7:40b.

The church is said to be "sanctified in Christ Jesus," "called to be holy," and is identified as part of the church universal. In these descriptions Paul defines the Corinthians and gives a prescription for what ails them, for they are said to be holy *in Christ,* not of themselves, and they are part of a larger whole of which they should not lose sight (similarly 1 Cor 12).

Verse 3 concludes the opening with Paul's normal greeting, "grace and peace."

Thanksgiving. Paul briefly raises the concerns of the letter in this thanksgiving (1:4–9)—the Corinthians' claim of an enriched status in speech, knowledge, and spiritual gifts. Given the content of the rest of the letter, one wonders how deeply the apostle perceived his tongue to be buried in his cheek here. Nevertheless, he identifies the period in which the Corinthians stand as a time of waiting for the "revealing" of the Lord Jesus Christ, and he expresses unflagging confidence in the power and faithfulness of God.

The Body of the Letter. This extends from 1:10 through 15:52. It contains a variety of material, so extensive as to preclude detailed consideration here. But generally the body of the letter falls into four large units.

1 Cor 1:10–4:21 takes up basic issues of Christian belief and the Corinthian situation. Paul argues that the gospel is not a new wisdom teaching that imparts information to those in the know and elevates them above the masses. Indeed to those seeking such "wisdom," the gospel ("the word of the cross") appears to be foolishness; but to those who hear, believe, and see that in the cross God acted to save the world, the gospel is the *power* of God. Notice 1:18:

> For the word of the cross to the ones who are perishing is folly,
> but to us who are being saved it is the power of God.

Paul names two groups (those perishing and those being saved) and specifies what the gospel is to each of them (folly or power). Strikingly in this juxtaposition he does not call the word of the cross "the wisdom of God" for those being saved; rather it is the power of God. Paul is saying that salvation comes from what God does, not from what humanity knows. Moreover, the perception of the gospel as folly or power reveals how God is dealing with groups of humans, not what humans know.

Paul labors to distance himself and his ministry from the Corinthian preoccupation with wisdom. He claims that he taught no wisdom, nor did he preach the gospel "with eloquent wisdom." Paul says he preached nothing more or less than Christ and him crucified, for the power of God at work in the cross of Christ is God's wisdom, though human wisdom evaluates it as foolishness.

With this Paul tells the Corinthians they have no wisdom of which to boast—for all other than the cross is folly to God. Thus the way the Corinthians approach the gospel bespeaks their spiritual immaturity. Paul says sadly that thinking themselves wise they are only fooling themselves.

1 Cor 5:1–11:1 is an extensive set of criticisms and directives. Here Paul comes down hard on the *boasting* being done by the various Corinthian factions. Boasting, he says, only tears down; it does not

build up the church. The behavior of some of the Corinthians is deplorable, but Paul is more concerned with the boasting about such behavior, for arrogance ostracizes and threatens the unity of the church. The directions Paul gives aim at unification and, in turn, the strengthening of the congregation.

In this portion of the body of the letter Paul speaks to the Corinthians' questions about sex, marriage, and food offered to idols. Unfortunately, Paul's advice is frequently misunderstood. For example, at 7:1 the RSV reads, "Now concerning the matters about which you wrote. It is well for a man not to touch a woman." Readers often take the second sentence to be Paul's primary desire, namely no sexual relations. Then the verses that follow 7:1 are taken as an exception. This interpretation is not completely erroneous, but some understanding of Paul's style of argumentation aids better comprehension. Here and throughout the letter (see esp. 6:12–13), Paul employs a technique for arguing that was common in his day among popular Hellenistic moralists, the Stoic-Cynic diatribe. Simply stated, in this style of argument one creates an artificial dialogue by quoting one's opponent and then offering a rebuttal to the quoted position. Thus understood, 7:1 may be paraphrased, "Now concerning the things of which you wrote, namely your saying, 'It is a good thing for a man not to touch a woman.' " This starting point puts 7:1 and much of the rest of this section in a different light from that usually cast on it by readers. Paul continues through 11:1 giving advice aimed at unifying the Christian community.

In 11:2–14:40 Paul explicates matters related to church order. As in the preceding material, his chief concern is the edification of the church. He insists worship should be orderly. The Lord's Supper should celebrate and be an occasion for congregational unity. Spiritual gifts are *all* for building up the church; they are not items to be compared for individual or group boasting—for love is the eternal element, and thereby the standard, of Christian behavior. Paul exposes the Corinthians' fallacious preoccupation with the flashier spiritual gifts which are used for little more than boasting. For example, Paul spends considerable time treating *glossolalia* or "speaking in tongues." The Corinthians apparently thought of *glossolalia* as "angel language or speech" (1 Cor 13:1). The sheer conspicuousness of "tongues" made it a gift with which the Corinthians were much impressed and for which they were particularly desirous (14:12). Then as now this phenomenon was little understood. Paul does not deny that *glossolalia* is a gift of the Spirit, but from his comments in 1 Cor 13–14, a sober reader should see that *glossolalia* was not something that Paul either encouraged or about which he normally cared. He bluntly plays *glossolalia* down (13:11; 14:5, 18) and offers guidelines for its regulation (14:6, 13, 26–33a). Paul clearly wants such behavior checked and kept in place. It is striking that Paul does not deny the validity of the experience of *glossolalia,* but he labors to deny the shallow theology and the self-centered use to which the Corinthians put "tongues." In short, for Paul *glossolalia* is not what some Corinthian Christians and many twentieth century "charismatic" Christians say, namely the indispensable sign of the Spirit. That role belongs to *love* (1 Cor 13). Thus 1 Cor 14:26 sounds the keynote of both this section and the body of the letter, "Let all things be for edification!"

The final portion of the letter's body, 15:1–52, gives eschatological instruction as a corrective to the Corinthian situation. Paul assumes that the Corinthians badly misunderstand the resurrection. It is neither immortality of the soul, as it was in popular Hellenistic philosophy, nor a timeless truth applicable to all of life's moments. Paul says the resurrection is an *event* that took place in proleptic form in God's raising of Jesus Christ from the dead. For Christians it is a future happening, to occur at Christ's coming, that is to be presently awaited.

Parenesis. The letter begins to close (16:1–18) with Paul's recital of his plans. He speaks of the Jerusalem collection, his own future travels, his dispatching of Timothy, and his conversation with Apollos. Verses 13–14 quickly recapitulate the basic directions given throughout the foregoing chapters, and vv. 15–18 single out those in Corinth worthy of special mention.

Closing. The letter ends in six moves. Greetings are passed (vv. 19–20). Paul signs the letter (v. 21). He pronounces a general anathema upon no one in particular (v. 22) and inscribes a primitive Christian eschatological cry, here transliterated into Greek from Aramaic, *marana tha* ("Come, our Lord!"). He pronounces a benediction of *grace* upon the Corinthians (v. 23) and then adds *his love*—an unusual element in Paul's letters (v. 24).

Paul's Advice to the Corinthians

Paul's letter is replete with sarcasm (e.g., 4:8–13). He is obviously upset by the developments in Corinth, but he still "loves" (16:24) the church there. Thus he labors to bring the Corinthians into line. He regards the situation as a symptom of the Corinthians' fundamental misunderstanding of the gospel, and so he confronts the cliques in Corinth for their spiritual arrogance that is destroying the community. He does this by disparaging the (human) wisdom that is esteemed by the Corinthians. Paul does not deny that wisdom exists (2:6), but he avers that it is not human wisdom, but God's revealed wisdom that matters. Paul juxtaposes human wisdom and the cross of Christ and suggests that human wisdom seeks to empty the cross of its power. Then he proclaims that God's power has made human wisdom irrelevant—the cross exposes it—since God's foolishness is greater than human wisdom and God's weakness is greater than human strength.

In arguing Paul relativizes everything with which the Corinthians seem concerned by saying that this world and its present form are passing away (2:6; 7:29–31). He denounces showy asceticism and bald, immoral licentiousness. He acknowledges that freedom and privilege are granted to Christians in the cross, God's powerful act for salvation; but Christian conduct should be a renunciation of one's privileges and an acceptance of the weak conscience of other members of the church and even of pagan observers.

Paul declares that the church must understand itself to be the one body of Christ, not as a bunch of empowered individuals or groups. Individualism and factionalism destroy both the individual and the church. Thus, on church order, Paul denounces without exception all behavior that seeks to demonstrate advanced religious insight and possession of outstanding spiritual gifts. There is to be no grading and comparing of spiritual gifts. Indeed at the end of 1 Cor 12 Paul gives a list of gifts that probably reverses the Corinthians' order of value. He teaches that no special gift proves God's presence—the only indispensable sign of the blessing of God's Spirit is love.

Theological Keys to 1 Corinthians

Throughout the letter Paul is concerned with promoting the unity of the flamboyant, fragmented Corinthian church. He exposes the folly and danger of human wisdom by juxtaposing it to God's power revealed in the cross (and resurrection) of Christ. Paul focuses on the cross, using it as the standard for Christian conduct in the interim after the death-and-resurrection and before the coming of Christ (1 Cor 10:11). Christians live in Christ—him crucified—hoping for his coming. While Christians have an assurance of inheriting the glory of the resurrection which is already a reality for Christ himself, they do not yet have a share of that glory, for Christ has not yet come to bring about their own resurrection transformation. Therefore Christians are not called to vanity and they do not possess spiritual superiority. Rather, the cross qualifies their current existence—establishing selfless sacrifice as the norm for life in the time between the whiles. In this interim the only cause for boasting by Christians is what God has done, is doing, and will do in Jesus Christ for the salvation of the world. Knowing this should free the Corinthians to love one another and to labor to build up the church.

BIBLIOGRAPHY

C. K. Barrett, *A Commentary on the First Epistle to the Corinthians* (HNTC; New York: Harper & Row, 1968).

H. Conzelmann, *1 Corinthians* (Hermeneia; Philadelphia: Fortress, 1975—German original 1969).

J. C. Hurd, *The Origin of 1 Corinthians* (rev. ed.; Macon: Mercer University, 1983).

J. Murphy-O'Connor, *1 Corinthians* (New Testament Message 10; Wilmington: Glazier, 1979).

Idem, St. Paul's Corinth (Good News Studies 6; Wilmington: Glazier, 1983).

2 Corinthians

This letter presents some of the most fascinating problems of interpretation found in the New Testament. Scholars have wrestled with this letter thoroughly, and in striving to understand this epistle it is helpful to call upon their efforts. That shall be done in the following pages. But even though we have occasion to discuss scholarship more extensively than elsewhere in this book, our primary goal is to grasp the meaning of 2 Corinthians, not to master interpretative theories—though they seem indispensable here.

Paul's Continuing Relationship to the Corinthians

As will become clear below, there are a variety of ways to understand what went on between Paul and the Corinthians after he wrote 1 Corinthians. All reconstructions of the story are related, however, to how one understands 2 Corinthians. What follows is as neutral a delineation of the events as is possible.

After writing 1 Corinthians Paul remained in Ephesus. He did, however, pay a brief second visit to Corinth, for 2 Cor 2:1; 12:14; and 13:1 refer to an impending third visit. The exact motivation for the second visit is difficult to determine, but 2 Cor 2:1, 5–11; 7:12; and 10:1–12 make it clear that the visit was unpleasant—Paul says he was treated badly (2:3, 5; 7:12). Moreover, newcomers had arrived in Corinth and under their influence some Corinthians were opposed to Paul. After his departure from Corinth Paul wrote a blistering letter to the Corinthians; he refers to this letter in 2 Cor 2:3–4, 9; and 7:8–12. He sent the letter to Corinth by Titus (2:13; 7:5–16). Paul was sufficiently distressed by the Corinthian situation that he did not remain in Ephesus but went to Troas and then set out for Macedonia to intercept Titus in order to learn about the outcome of Titus' visit in his behalf. Finding Titus, he learned that the letter, and Titus' intervention, had been effective. Paul's anguished letter had moved the Corinthians to a repentant godly grief (7:5–11), and Paul and the Corinthians were reconciled. After learning of the reconciliation Paul wrote to the Corinthians.

The Problem(s) That Elicited This Letter

As noted, 2 Corinthians reveals that sometime after Paul wrote 1 Corinthians outsiders arrived in Corinth. The outsiders are preachers, and their message is that Christianity is a strange, vitally renewed Judaism. These people were Jewish Christians, for they bragged about their heritage, saying they were "Hebrews, Israelites, the *sperma Abraam* (Abraham's seed), and servants of Christ" (11:22–23). It is striking, however, that 2 Corinthians does not mention the law or circumcision; thus it is safe to conclude that these newcomers are not the same people Paul opposed in Galatians. Rather than focusing on the law and its observation these Jewish Christians seem concerned with possessing the power to work miracles, for the substance of Paul's argument in 2 Cor 2–6 is that divine power comes out of God, not out of human beings. As 2 Cor 4:7 says, "We (Paul and his companions) have this treasure (the gospel ministry) in earthen vessels (the limited condition of being human) so that the extraordinary nature of the power may be God's and not out of ourselves." Moreover, Paul's sardonic title for the Corinthian newcomers is "super-apostles," a description that plays off the claims they make for themselves (11:5; 12:11). Paul's use of "super-apostles" is pejorative, but this may have been the newcomers' designation for themselves. Whatever the origin of "super-apostles" we shall use this name for those people who came to Corinth.

Those Whom Paul Opposes in 2 Corinthians

If one reads carefully between the lines, a picture of the super-apostles emerges. Coming from Jewish Christian circles they were like the other Hellenistic religious propagandists of the day. They had a flashy, obviously powerful style of ministry—powerful proclamation and powerful deeds. Their capabilities were documented (3:1) and they backed up their claims (3:5) with an allegorical interpretation of the Old Testament they insisted was authoritative (3:4–18). They came to the Corinthians, portraying themselves as some kind of divine men by appealing to Moses as their prototype in powerful ministry (3:7–18). They probably recounted the miracles of Jesus and claimed that Christianity was a miracle religion, for in conducting their ministry they called themselves "servants of Christ" (11:23). They claimed (3:5) they *had* power and probably suggested that they could hand it over to their hearers (4:2). Moreover, they bragged about their mystical experiences and spiritual prayers (12:1–9). Compared to themselves the super-apostles said Paul was worldly and weak (10:1–2).

The Corinthians took the super-apostles in, and the super-apostles *took in* the Corinthians and set some of them against Paul. The ploy of the super-apostles is discernible from Paul's comments. In addition to boasting of their own abilities they have criticized Paul for his failures as an apostle: he has *no credentials* as they do (3:1–3), he is *not impressive* in words, deeds, or presence (10:1–12, esp. vv. 1 and 10), and he is *without depth* of spiritual experience (12:1–13). They compared Paul unfavorably with themselves (10:12), saying he was meek when face to face but bold in his letter (10:1). They made their point by saying Paul was so timid that he did not dare demand his rightful support as an apostle (11:7).

The Structure of Paul's Letter

Any reader of 2 Corinthians sees that the letter has at least three distinct sections. Chapters 1–7 discuss the reconciliation of Paul and the Corinthians; chapters 8–9 give directions concerning the collection for the poor in Jerusalem; chapters 10–13 are a scorching tirade laden with sarcasm and vituperation aimed at a rebellious congregation.

Within these major sections, however, scholars recognize structural anomalies in the form of several sharp, atypical breaks. At two places (between 2:13 and 14; between 7:4 and 5) it is difficult, if not impossible, to follow the transition; and even more problematic is the seeming interruption of 6:14–7:1 that produces sheer discontinuity between 6:13 and 14 and between 7:1 and 2. Moreover, chapters 8 and

9 seem redundant if not discontinuous and illogical together. Finally, chapters 10–13 begin after a sharp break from 9:15 and on the whole are nearly impossible to reconcile with what is said in 7:5–16.

These literary problems inspire a series of interpretations that attempt to make sense of the material in 2 Corinthians. As will be evident, each *literary* theory is bound to a particular *historical* reconstruction. We shall consider several of these, taking prominent, available works as examples of the various positions. (The bibliography gives full references.)

W. G. Kümmel sees the letter falling into the three major parts mentioned above (1–7; 8–9; 10–13). He admits that the parts are not clearly related, and he argues that the breaks and the illogical transitions are the results of interruptions Paul suffered in the process of dictating the letter.

Anyone who has ever dictated a letter and been interrupted while doing so will find this explanation weak, for it is a simple matter to turn to the secretary and say, "Now where was I before I was interrupted?" Thus many scholars accept more complicated explanations of the difficulties in 2 Corinthians.

C. K. Barrett posits that 2 Corinthians is a composite of two letters by Paul that were joined by a later editor, not the apostle. Barrett suggests that Paul paid the painful visit to Corinth, after which he wrote the anguished letter to the Corinthians. Paul sent this letter which is now lost by Titus as messenger. Titus returned and brought news of the Corinthian situation, and Paul wrote 2 Cor 1–9, a letter of reconciliation, to defend his apostolic office and to discuss the collection. Titus bore this letter to Corinth, but found the situation precarious. He returned with a bad report for Paul, who then wrote 2 Cor 10–13.

This explanation is not completely satisfactory, for it does not deal with the internal tensions throughout chapters 1–9. Moreover, it relies upon the fabricated misunderstanding by Titus of the Corinthian situation in order to explain how chapters 10–13 could possibly follow 2 Cor 1–9.

C. M. Connick is among scholars who reverse the two letter theory just described. He understands the painful letter mentioned in 2 Cor 2:4; 7:8–12 to be chapters 10–13. The scenario he projects is this: The problem addressed in 1 Corinthians persisted and was complicated by the arrival of Jewish Christian outsiders. Paul paid the painful visit to Corinth and subsequently wrote 2 Cor 10–13. This letter effected a reconciliation, and subsequently Paul wrote chapters 1–9. Connick explains the seeming discontinuities at 6:13–14 and 7:1–2 by labeling 6:14–7:1 an interpolation. He judges that in assembling the letter now called 2 Corinthians, an editor preserved a fragment of the earlier Pauline letter mentioned in 1 Cor 5:9–11 by inserting it into the body of Paul's letter in chapters 1–9.

R. A. Spivey and D. M. Smith advocate a similar, though slightly more elaborate form of this theory. They begin, however, from a different point. The problem in Corinth was caused by the super-apostles. Paul learned of this and made his second trip to Corinth, the painful visit. Then Paul wrote chapters 10–13, sending this message by Titus. The angry letter brought about a reconciliation. Hearing this good news Paul wrote 2 Cor 1–8 in defense of his apostolic office and advocating the collection. At a later time he followed up on the collection with 2 Cor 9. Spivey and Smith also view 6:14–7:1 as an interpolation by the later editor, perhaps from the letter mentioned in 1 Corinthians.

These explanations are not persuasive, for they still do not account for all the difficulties. What of the rough transitions between 2:13 and 14 and between 7:4 and 5? And why would Paul reiterate a defense for his apostleship when he and the Corinthians are already reconciled?

R. K. Bultmann also operates with the idea of two Pauline letters that were joined by a later editor, but he accounts for the literary tensions that the foregoing theories could not resolve by positing a more elaborate reconstruction scheme. He argues that after a painful visit to Corinth Paul wrote his anguished letter which is now preserved in 2 Cor 2:14–7:4 (6:14–7:1 is an interpolation); 9; and 10–13. This castigating letter produced a reconciliation, and then Paul wrote a letter of reconciliation now found in 1:1–2:13; 7:5–16; and 8.

While this suggestion explains the literary awkwardness of 2 Corinthians, scholars do not widely accept the reconstruction. The elements that Bultmann suggests formed the painful letter are judged by critics to be unbelievably diversified. For example, the somber, logical tone of 2:14–7:4 is unlike the anger and sarcasm of 10–13. And is it likely that Paul would have included instructions on the collection (chapter 9) in a letter where he is fighting to stave off a mutiny? Indeed, is not the optimistic tone of 2 Cor 9 completely different from either 2:14–7:4 or 10–13? Thus interpreters continue to examine 2 Corinthians.

G. Bornkamm and D. Georgi offer similar, more elaborate literary-historical reconstructions to account for the various interpretative problems. Though their theories are not exactly the same we shall consider them together, for the only real difference between their suggestions regards 2 Cor 8. Both understand that while he was in Ephesus Paul learned of the presence of the super-apostles in Corinth and wrote 2:14–7:4 (minus 6:14–7:1, which both judge to be a non-Pauline interpolation) as an apology for his apostolic authority and activity. This letter had no effect, so Paul went to Corinth (2:1; 12:14; 13:1), paying a visit that was a complete failure. Paul returned to Ephesus and dashed off the severe letter, chapters 10–13, and sent it by Titus to Corinth. Paul went to Troas to await Titus, and when he did not soon arrive Paul went to Macedonia and met Titus. Titus brought news of the Corinthians' grief and the reconciliation between them and the apostle, and Paul wrote 1:1–2:13; 7:5–16. Bornkamm suggests that 2 Cor 8 fits well at the end of this letter of reconciliation, but Georgi holds that Paul sent Titus with this note on the collection at a later time. Both suggest that chapter 9 came from Paul at a still later date.

It is impossible to prove or refute this resourceful hypothesis. Other scholars have subjected the theory to rigorous criticism. Kümmel is representative in posing two questions against this elaborate thesis:

(1) Does the text as transmitted compel one to assume that material has been combined secondarily? Kümmel claims there is no such reason, but it is striking that he has to create and rely upon upsetting interruptions in the process of dictation in order to account for the illogical transitions, contrasting tones, and otherwise inscrutable flow of this letter. Thus Kümmel is not persuasive when he says there are no reasons to assume the secondary combining of material to form 2 Corinthians, for he cannot demonstrate the unity of the whole.

(2) Can a convincing motive be perceived for the combining of material as it has been transmitted in 2 Corinthians? Kümmel believes this question raises the decisive objection, since no completely convincing motive for the editing of 2 Corinthians into its present form has been put forward. Nevertheless, to quote Barrett, who basically

agrees with Kümmel, "It may be that no limit should be set to the stupidity of the editors, and one cannot expect always to understand their motives." Moreover, a better question than Kümmel's so-called decisive one is, "Is there a theory that makes better sense of *all* the evidence than does the simple acceptance of 2 Corinthians as it is handed down in the tradition?" In response to this question, I would judge that Bornkamm and Georgi have supplied more gratifying answers than Kümmel and those who hold the other positions described above. The strength of their seemingly elaborate reconstruction is that *it makes sense of the text from the text*—it suggests nothing to have happened that is not reported in the text.

Thus with minor adjustments, we shall work with this hypothesis in studying the content of the letter. Because none of the letters probably survives intact, the usual format is abandoned. The following sketch delineates the order in which we shall take up the material in 2 Corinthians:

1. Paul sent Titus and two unnamed brothers to Corinth with instructions concerning the collection, namely 2 Cor 8.

2. These emissaries returned with news of an attack on Paul in Corinth by some newcomers. Paul then wrote a letter defending his apostleship, namely 2 Cor 2:14–7:4 (minus the interpolation in 6:14–7:1 from an earlier letter mentioned in 1 Cor 5:9).

3. Paul paid his painful visit to Corinth, mentioned in 2 Cor 2:2; 12:14; and 13:1, and as a result of this experience he wrote a tearful letter that grieved the Corinthians and brought a reconciliation between them and him, namely 2 Cor 10–13.

4. Paul learned from Titus of the reconciliation and wrote a warm letter acknowledging the restoration, namely 2 Cor 1:1–2:13 and 7:5–16.

5. Subsequently Paul wrote another letter about the collection, namely 2 Cor 9. This letter could have been carried along with the letter of reconciliation or could have been sent at a later time.

2 Corinthians 8. This chapter forms a letter of recommendation for Titus and two unnamed brothers, the three of whom act as Paul's agents in working to assemble the collection from the non-Palestinian churches for the poor saints in Jerusalem. As noted above, Paul was concerned with this collection because he saw in it a means for con-

2 CORINTHIANS

A letter about the collection	Chapter 8
A letter defending Paul's apostleship	2:14–7:4 (minus 6:14–7:1)
A stinging communication	Chapters 10–13
A letter of reconciliation	1:1–2:13 + 7:5–16
Another collection letter	Chapter 9
A Pauline fragment	6:14–7:1

cretizing the unity of the law-observant and the non-law-observant congregations; it brought together the givers and the recipients in a common acknowledgement of their oneness in Christ.

Paul holds up the Macedonian congregations to the Corinthians as examples; in spite of adverse conditions they have been models of generosity. But the real appeal he makes is a call for the Corinthians to give graciously as the Lord Jesus Christ did by making a selfless sacrifice out of genuine love for humanity (8:9).

2 Corinthians 2:14–7:4. In his defense of himself, or, better, in defending his apostleship, Paul works to distinguish the true experience of God's power from flashy success. He argues that God's power must be understood on the model of the Christ-event, especially the cross. This alone reveals what is eternal. By juxtaposing God's work in Christ to the activity of the super-apostles, Paul demonstrates that flashy power is transient, not eternal.

Paul defends himself by implying that the super-apostles are "peddlers" of God's word (2:17). In contrast Paul is sincere, for he (unlike them?) is commissioned by God. Whereas they have letters of recommendation, Paul has his establishing of the church at Corinth. Whereas they claim power is in their possession (3:5), Paul says all he has is from God; and, moreover, the flashy is fading (3:7). Paul implies that the super-apostles are "underhanded"; they are cunning and tamper with God's word (by adding their power program); and, in short, they preach themselves (4:2–5). But Paul does not preach himself; he preaches Jesus Christ as Lord, with himself as servant of the Corinthian church for Jesus' sake (4:5).

Paul insists that the limitations of human existence characterize his ministry, for this alone shows saving power to be God's (4:7–18). Paul does not win converts by listing his successes; rather he is afflicted, perplexed, and persecuted (4:8). Yet, through it all God sustains him and thereby manifests the life of Jesus—his suffering, death, and the hope of his resurrection—in Paul's own flesh (4:11; 6:4–10). Paul says he dies so the Corinthians may live (4:11–12, 15), and his ministry has the character of suffering service (6:3–10) because he now knows Christ in the context of God's new creation (5:16–20).

Paul concludes his defense by making an appeal to the Corinthians to open their hearts to him. He expresses his pride in them and his confidence that they will do what he asks. Unfortunately, that chapters 10–13 follow this defense (whether one approaches the letter as handed down in tradition or as reconstructed in the current hypothesis) indicates that Paul was at least temporarily disappointed.

2 Corinthians 10–13. Here Paul launches a sizzling tirade against the ways with which the Corinthians are so taken. His line is similar to that of the previous letter, namely that his style of ministry and his theology are of a piece and reflect his focus on the Christ-event. Paul says that his refusal to engage in a showy ministry is not a sign of his worldliness; indeed it is the opposite. He refrains from displays of power, ministering in and through affliction, so that true divine power, as revealed in Jesus Christ, may work through him. He is in this manner God's agent in cosmic battle, not a worldly war (10:3–4). Paul exposes the inappropriateness of comparing, measuring, and boasting as the super-apostles do. This activity is typical of self-centeredness (10:12). Therefore, if he boasts, Paul says it is of the Lord, not his own accomplishments (10:17–18).

In chapter 11 Paul begins to engage in what he calls "a little foolishness." He answers the criticism that he did not extract his livelihood from the Corinthians because he was too timid to demand his due (11:7–11). His foolishness is sarcasm in 11:1–11, but at 11:12 Paul declares his intention to undermine the super-apostles. He strikes a bold, seemingly imprudent chord, calling the super-apostles "false prophets" and "deceitful workers" who disguise themselves as apostles of Christ when they are really Satan's servants (11:13–15). Paul returns to his sarcasm with a satirical, ironical "fool's boast" in 11:16–12:10. Herein he shows his scorn for the duped Corinthians and the super-apostles. He issues threats and presses up to and past the limits of good taste. He boasts, but rather than enumerate his own successful deeds in missionary work he catalogues the crises and disasters he has experienced. He concludes chapter 11 with the story of his cowardly escape from Damascus (11:32–33). He continues in chapter 12 by distancing himself from the claims of the super-apostles to spiritual depth. He boasts of his own spiritual experiences, but he is not straightforward about it, for ironically he is not quite sure about the identity of the "spiritual man" whose mystical visions and revelations he reports. Finally, he adds sarcastically that when he prayed for God miraculously to remove the thorn in his flesh he got no powerful results. Indeed, God did not do that for which he prayed; rather God said, "My grace is enough for you, for (my) power is fulfilled in weakness" (12:9). Paul's point is that his weakness allows a distinction to be made between his own pitiful efforts and the gracious, sustaining power of God.

Paul closes the letter by issuing a few bracing warnings. The sarcasm is gone. Paul tells the Corinthians of his plans to visit them and of his hope that the strong letter will set things straight so that he will not have to be severe when he comes to them for a third time.

2 Corinthians 1:1–2:13; 7:5–16. Paul acknowledges the reconciliation of which he learned after Titus returned from going to the Corinthians with Paul's severe letter. Paul expresses his pleasure in a warm, passionate way. Moreover, in a civilized fashion he now addresses a criticism the Corinthians had made, namely his changing of his announced travel plans. This earlier change in plans must have exacerbated the former situation, for Paul wants to clear up any lingering misunderstanding. The apostle also instructs the Corinthians to "forgive and comfort" the very person who offended Paul during his second visit to Corinth (2:5–11).

2 Corinthians 9. This is Paul's final (preserved) word to the Corinthians about the collection. He admonishes them to sow as they would reap, surely with abundance. They are to give cheerfully, remembering that God supplies their needs. They will be rewarded for their giving, for it will produce thanksgiving to God on the part of the poor saints in Jerusalem who will receive this relief.

An Interpolation: 2 Cor 6:14–7:1. This fragment which breaks roughly into the flow of Paul's defense of his apostleship in 2:14–7:4 appears to be a part of an earlier letter mentioned in 1 Cor 5:9. These verses advise the readers to avoid defilement. Paul explained in 1 Corinthians that he meant this advice to apply only to the internal life of the congregation, but some Corinthians thought he spoke about dealings with non-Christians. After reading the passage and noticing the obscure metaphorical character of the communication, one should sympathize with the Corinthians who misperceived Paul's exact point.

Paul's Advice to the Corinthians

Paul claims to write to the Corinthians, even in his most agitated state, for the good of the church, not in defense of himself (12:19). Though the super-apostles have sought to embarrass Paul with their critique of his ministry, he says God, not they, will humble him. Moreover, this divine humbling will not be the faulting of Paul personally; it will be the embarrassment Paul will suffer should the Corinthians continue in their erroneous ways (12:21).

With regard to his adversaries in Corinth Paul says the super-apostles only know Christ "according to the flesh" (2 Cor 5:16). This is a literal translation of Paul's Greek phrase, *kata sarka*. The RSV renders the words "from a human point of view," but this misses Paul's point. He speaks here from his apocalyptic perspective, saying that the super-apostles view Christ out of the realm and in the power of the present evil age (as Paul once had but no longer did—see 5:16). If they regarded Christ in the context of the "new creation" (5:17) they would understand the significance of his death—"he died in behalf of all in order that those who live might live no longer for themselves but for the one who died and was raised for them" (5:15). Then they would understand that in the interim between the crucifixion-resurrection and coming of Christ the character of Christian life is stamped by the cross, for Christians live in this present mingled time afflicted by Satan's forces but sustained by the saving power of God. But Paul says the super-apostles claim to have raw power at their disposal, so they are really preaching themselves (4:5), commending themselves (10:12), and serving Satan (11:13–15).

Paul says that the character of his own ministry, not that of the super-apostles, is in conformity with the gospel. He tells the Corinthians to examine themselves to see whether they are holding to their faith (13:5). If their lives conform to Christ's own loving selfless sacrifice (8:9) then Christ is in them; if not, he is not (13:5).

Theological Keys to 2 Corinthians

Paul is concerned throughout 2 Corinthians to deny that humans possess God's power and manipulate it at their will, for God's treasure is in earthen vessels (4:7). By claiming to have power the super-apostles reveal they are not in the realm of the new creation, for they still know Christ "according to the flesh" (5:16–17). Paul on the other hand knows that Christians, who are currently in the realm of the new creation, live conformed to the cross of the Lord Jesus Christ—afflicted, but sustained by the grace of God (11:9). Thus Paul can say, "For when I am weak, then I am strong"—indicating that as he yields himself to God in trusting obedience he is sustained through affliction and God prevails (12:10). Moreover, knowing this, Paul does not gloat over his ability to withstand hardships, for God does the sustaining; thus if he boasts, Paul boasts of the Lord (10:17–18). All Christians should do the same.

BIBLIOGRAPHY

C. K. Barrett, *A Commentary on the Second Epistle to the Corinthians* (HNTC; New York: Harper & Row, 1973).

G. Bornkamm, *Paul* (New York: Harper & Row, 1971) esp. 244–46.

R. Bultmann, *The Second Letter to the Corinthians* (Minneapolis: Augsburg, 1985—German original 1976 from lectures given in 1940 and 1952).

C. M. Connick, *The New Testament* (2d ed.; Belmont, Cal.: Wadsworth, 1978).

V. P. Furnish, *II Corinthians* (AB 32A; Garden City: Doubleday, 1984).

D. Georgi, *The Opponents of Paul in 2 Corinthians* (Philadelphia: Fortress, 1986—revision of German original from 1964).

Idem, "Corinthians, Second Letter to the," *IDBSup* 183–86.

R. A. Spivey and D. M. Smith, *Anatomy of the New Testament* (3d ed.; New York: Macmillan, 1982).

Romans

Called the Eternal City or the City of Seven Hills, Rome, in Paul's day, was the capital and by far the most important city in the Roman Empire. Centuries earlier Rome had been a set of rural hamlets located on the eastern bank of the Tiber River. The area was attractive because of its elevation above the marshy and malaria-plagued lowlands of the surrounding region, the Campagna. In the eighth century B.C. Etruscan invaders from the northwest (legend names Romulus and fixes the date at 753 B.C.) overran the rural hill settlements and subsequently unified the communities into a city-state. Etruscan domination continued until about 500 B.C. when the Romans threw off the foreign rulers and established the Roman Republic. During the republican era Rome emerged as a major world power. The Republic lasted about four hundred years, until the formation of the First Triumvirate in 60 B.C. From that group, by 48 B.C., Julius Caesar had emerged as the acknowledged master of Rome. His advent (60–48 B.C.) and tenure as Caesar (48–44 B.C.) were brief, but the effects of his reign marked Rome's character permanently. Rome was now not merely the capital city of an enormous military power; it was the cultural center of the extended Mediterranean world as well.

Julius Caesar's rule brought to an end the old Roman Republic and laid the foundation of the subsequent Roman Empire. His assassination was followed initially by anarchy and then by the formation of a Second Triumvirate. From this arrangement Caesar's nephew, Octavian—entitled Augustus by the Roman senate—emerged as the ruler of Rome; indeed, he became the first emperor of Rome. His reign (31 B.C.–A.D. 14) began a two hundred year long period of peace, the *Pax Romana,* in which the Empire prospered.

Paul was most likely born during the reign of Octavian, and he labored as an apostle when Tiberius (A.D. 14–37), Caligula (A.D. 37–41), Claudius (A.D. 41–54), and Nero (A.D. 54–68) ruled. Though these emperors were far less talented than either Caesar or Octavian, the Empire enjoyed the benefits of its sound formative years and Rome, the city, steadily grew in size and influence. In the first century the peoples of the diverse Roman provinces moved in large numbers to the capital city in order to be at the center of politics, commerce, travel, and culture. Indeed all roads did lead to Rome, and so we should not be surprised to learn that the apostle wrote to the Christians in Rome about his own plans to visit the capital city.

Nevertheless, in striking ways this letter is distinct from Paul's other letters. It is addressed to a church (or churches) founded by neither Paul nor one of his missionary colleagues. Moreover, Paul had never visited this community of Christians; yet he wrote them the longest of his preserved letters. In turn, other distinctive features of this letter are perhaps intelligible precisely because Paul did not have first-hand knowledge of the Roman church. For example, (1) the tone of Romans is more formal, reflective, and even more neutral here than in the other letters, (2) Paul's style is closer to that of first century Jewish apologetics than is his pattern of expression elsewhere, and (3) Paul uses early Christian traditional material in Romans that does not appear in his other letters (more on these features below). The apostle's reserved manner and balanced reflection in Romans on matters that he discusses in a more agitated state in other letters lead many to describe this letter as Paul's most profound theological expression.

Paul's Relationship to the Roman Church

In order to comprehend Paul's relationship to the Roman Christians one must grapple with two problems, one related to the text of Paul's letter and another concerning the history of Christianity at Rome.

First, consider the textual problem. Romans is preserved in three distinct versions or forms: Rom 1–14 + the doxology in what is now Rom 16:25–27; Rom 1–15 + Rom 16:25–27; and Rom 1–16:23 (sometimes + 16:25–27). Scholars universally recognize that the shortest form of Romans (Rom 1–14 + doxology) is a truncated version of the letter, likely produced by the second century (heretical) Christian Marcion who took exception to the praise of the Old Testament in Rom 15:4 and the subsequent Old Testament quotations. Therefore the debatable issues are whether Rom 16:1–23 was part of Paul's letter to Rome and whether the doxology (Rom 16:25–27) is Pauline at all. Because the doxology appears in no fewer than six different places in the manuscript evidence and because of the non-Pauline character of the praise, scholars generally understand these verses to come from someone other than Paul—perhaps Marcion who abbreviated the original letter. Thus the real issue among scholars is whether Rom 16:1–23 was directed to Rome. The existence of both a fifteen and a sixteen chapter version of Romans and careful analysis of Rom 16 *per se* leads many scholars to argue that Paul wrote Rom 1–15, sending the letter to Rome *and* sending a copy of Rom 1–15 + 16:1–23 to Ephesus by Phoebe. The line of this argument is that Paul is not likely to have known as many people in Rome as he greets in Rom 16 (twenty-six); moreover, Prisca and Aquila are named in Rom 16:3, and from 1 Cor 16:19 one knows the couple was in Ephesus in the mid-50s; further, Epaenetus is referred to in Rom 16:5 as the first convert in *Asia;* and finally, Paul's appeal in Rom 16:17 ("to watch out for the ones creating dissensions and scandals against the teaching that you learned; stay away from them") seems heavy-handed in relation to a church he did not know. Rather than make a decision at this point about the accuracy of this attractive hypothesis, we turn to the second major problem mentioned above, namely the history of Christianity in Rome. By turning to this topic, one garners further data for making a prudent decision about the original purpose of Rom 16.

Ironically Paul's letter to Rome is the earliest indisputable reference to Christianity in Rome. His writing reveals that there was a church there in the mid-to-late 50s. Drawing inferences from other later sources scholars conclude that Christianity came to Rome at least in the 40s, and possibly earlier. The evidence is as follows: The Roman historian Suetonius, writing in the early second century, records that Claudius "expelled Jews from Rome because of their constant disturbances at the instigation of Chrestus" (*Life of Claudius* 25.4). Then in Acts 18:2 one learns that in Corinth Paul met and lived with Aquila and Priscilla (the Prisca and Aquila of Paul's letters) who had "recently come from Italy . . . because Claudius had commanded all the Jews to leave Rome." As noted above, it is best to understand that Prisca and Aquila were already Christians when Paul met them, for there is nothing in the Acts account or the letters of Paul to suggest otherwise. Viewing these bits of information together, scholars conclude that the "Chrestus" to whom Suetonius refers was not a particular Roman troublemaker—notice that Suetonius does not say "one named Chrestus" or "a certain Chrestus"—rather the name is a garbled reference to "Christ." Indeed in the second century both Christ and Christian were frequently (mis-)spelled with an "e" rather than an "i." Thus scholars argue that Christianity made its way to Rome at least in the 40s *among the Jews.*

Some confirmation for this interpretation of the arrival of Christianity in Rome comes from Ambrosiaster, a late fourth century Latin commentator on Paul's letters. In his introductory remarks to Romans, Ambrosiaster writes, "The Romans had received the faith of Christ, albeit according to the Jewish rite, although they saw no sign of mighty works nor any of the apostles" (*Corpus Scriptorum Ecclesiasticorum Latinorum* 81.1 or *Patrologiae Latina* 17.48). By this remark Ambrosiaster means only that Christianity arrived in Rome among the Jews there before any apostle ever visited the city, for he knows of the later presence of Paul in Rome.

But what does it mean to say that early Roman Christianity had a Jewish bent? Formerly scholars distinguished quite facilely between "Jewish Christianity" and "Gentile Christianity," but recent work by R. E. Brown shows that such a distinction is both simplistic and misleading. It is possible to distinguish at least four different types of early Jewish Christians based upon their differing attitudes toward Jewish observances. Moreover, each type engaged in missionary activity among the Gentiles and made different demands of their Gentile converts. (In what follows I modify Brown's categories somewhat.) (1) Some Jewish Christians insisted upon full observance of the law and the practice of circumcision for both Jewish and Gentile Christians—e.g., the circumcision party of Acts 11 and the "false brethren" of Gal 2. (2) Other Jewish Christians did not demand that their Gentile converts be circumcised, but only that they keep a few Jewish observances—e.g., James and Peter according to Acts 15. (3) Still other Jewish Christians demanded of Gentile converts neither circumcision nor keeping any Jewish observances—Paul usually fits here. (4) Finally some Jewish Christians abandoned all Jewish observances and came to manifest an overtly hostile attitude toward Jewish practices— e.g., the Hellenists of Acts 6 and 11 *and* Paul when upset, as he is in Galatians.

For the purposes of this study the question is: *What kind of Jewish Christianity, making what sort of Gentile converts, existed in Rome prior to Paul's writing to the Romans?* There is little "Christian" evidence for answering this question. Rather one achieves some insight into the history of Christianity in Rome by observing that Roman Judaism in the first century was strongly tied to Jerusalem. The majority of Roman Jews (some forty to fifty thousand persons) came originally from Palestine and Syria and continued to look to the East as "home." If this is the case for Judaism one may suspect that the same situation could have characterized early Roman Jewish Christianity. Thus one would expect to find in Rome the more conservative attitude toward Jewish practices that characterized Jerusalem Christianity under the domination of Peter and James of Jerusalem. Indeed by understanding that Roman Christianity had close ties with the Jerusalem church, which was more conservative than Paul, one can understand (a) Paul's extensive consideration of the Jews in Rom 9–11 and his careful discussion of the relation of Jews and Gentiles throughout much of the rest of the letter and (b) Ambrosiaster's description of early Roman Christianity.

We may now return to consider whether Rom 16:1–23 was directed to Rome. In light of all factors I would join those scholars who judge that these verses were originally part of Paul's letter to Rome. First, precisely because he had never been to Rome Paul wrote greeting everyone he knew there. Second, he knew so many Roman Christians because (a) some of those whom he met on the mission field in the eastern Mediterranean moved to Rome as was common in the first century and (b) others, like Prisca and Aquila, who were banished from Rome by Claudius returned to their homes there (property was not necessarily lost due to banishment) after the death of Claudius in A.D. 54. Third, Rom 16:17 may be a kind of reverse-psychology: Paul knew some conservative Jewish Christians, and their Gentile converts in Rome had questions about his orthodoxy, so through this letter he laid out his position, arguing in the style of Jewish apologetics and citing primitive (Jerusalem?) Jewish Christian traditions extensively;

thus he can admonish the Roman Christians to avoid possible heretics, for clearly he is not one!

The Situation That Elicited This Letter

From the time of Melanchthon in the first half of the sixteenth century to as recent an interpreter as A. Nygren in 1944, commentators have described Romans as Paul's *christianae religionis compendium*. But with the development of the historical-critical method for the study of scripture, scholars came to recognize that each of the New Testament texts was written by the early church to serve its needs—in other words, the books of the New Testament were written by specific authors to particular audiences with concrete concerns. Yet Romans escaped the results of this insight longer than any other book. Why were scholars so slow in turning to study this letter from the historical-critical perspective? Perhaps, as noted, because Paul did not found the Roman church and when he wrote to Christians there he had never visited the city; perhaps also because of the formal tone of the letter.

When the historical-critical method began to have an impact on the interpretation of Romans, it produced contemporary contributions to the study of the letter of two types. Without engaging in critical debate it is well to survey the range of these interpretations. First, some scholars argue that in Romans *Paul is occupied primarily with his own concerns*. T. W. Manson, for example, contends that Paul gives in Romans a summary of his theology and practical positions. Similarly G. Bornkamm holds that in Romans Paul offers his "last will and testament"—that is, Romans is more than a summary, for therein Paul lifts his thoughts from their previous contexts in controversies in which he has been embroiled and moves them to a new level of abstraction. E. Fuchs does not perceive the letter to be so abstract as do Manson and Bornkamm, but he still maintains that Paul is preoccupied with his own forthcoming trip to Jerusalem. Thus Paul writes to Rome but his "secret addressees" are the Jerusalem Christians, for Paul's remarks to Rome are more fitting for the situation he will face in Jerusalem than for an unknown (to Paul) situation in Rome. Second, other scholars argue that in Romans *Paul is occupied primarily with the concerns of the Roman church*. Taking this line W. Marxsen avers that Paul wrote Romans to deal with the Jew/Gentile

issue at Rome that was a serious problem there. Marxsen understands
the Claudius edict of A.D. 49 to be an expulsion of Jewish Christians.
This act left the church in the hands of the Gentile Christians. With
Claudius' death in A.D. 54 the Roman Jewish Christians returned
home and a struggle for leadership ensued between the groups. G.
Klein agrees that Paul is focusing on the situation in Rome, but he
argues from Rom 15:20 that Paul wrote to prepare Rome for his visit
which he planned because he was concerned to go to Rome and provide that church with an apostolic base or foundation.

With such different opinions, all of which are more or less plau-
sible, being held by responsible scholars, how should one understand
the historical situation that motivated Paul to write to Rome? Perhaps
the "truth" lies somewhere between these two extremes, so that Paul
is not occupied strictly with either his own concerns or the concerns
of the Roman church. Instead there may be more factors than one
operating, and Paul may be simultaneously concerned with his forthcoming journey to Jerusalem and the situation in the church at Rome.

By gathering some of the threads of evidence examined thus far,
one may weave a tapestry that elaborates Paul's motives for writing
Romans. Paul is most likely in Corinth at the time of his writing—
regardless of the text one concludes Paul directed to Rome (Rom 1–
15 or Rom 1–16); for in Rom 16:1 (part of the original letter or part
of a note added to a copy of Romans that was sent elsewhere) Paul
commends Phoebe of Cenchreae, one of the port cities of Corinth.
The apostle is facing his forthcoming trip to Jerusalem with the assembled collection (15:25–26). While we read the grave danger we
know existed (from Acts) back into the mind of Paul as a premonition,
there is nothing in Romans to suggest that Paul expected a terrible
outcome for this trip. He certainly takes the trip seriously (15:30–32),
for he is pensive, even somber, throughout the whole letter and in
Rom 15 he acknowledges the possible danger in Jerusalem. But Paul
seems optimistic (15:24), perhaps because of the past sustaining by
God which he has experienced (see 2 Cor, esp, 12:7–10). Indeed expecting the best, Paul looks past Jerusalem not only to Rome, but he
even articulates his plans for future missionary work in the West, in
Spain (15:24, 28, 32). From what Paul writes, perhaps one should
understand that he wished to use Rome as a base in the West much
as he had used Antioch in the East, another church he did not found.

Moreover, with many friends in Rome (assuming Rom 16 is addressed to Rome), Paul probably knew the situation there. Furthermore, if Jerusalem and Rome were close in their attitudes and religious sensibilities, it was appropriate for Paul, when addressing Rome, to rehearse the arguments he would use in Jerusalem; for the Roman Christians might have many of the same reservations about Paul that some Christians and Jews in Jerusalem had. Thus to enjoy a good reception in Rome Paul lays out his thinking on controversial issues with which he has been involved in order to assuage any Roman anxiety or suspicion. Furthermore, he calls for support from the Romans not only for when he comes to them, but he requests their prayers for the trip to Jerusalem (15:30–33). Finally, by greeting everyone he knows in Rome, Paul identifies himself with a number of persons whom the Romans know personally and who may attest to the trustworthiness of the apostle as a servant of Christ.

Those Whom Paul Addresses and Their Theology

In light of the issues considered so far it should be obvious that Paul has no opponents in Rome. His letter does not seek to correct erroneous ways. He does give advice to the "strong" and the "weak," but these are Christians with differing religious sensibilities, not factions in the church engaged in comparing and boasting. Indeed Paul says of the Roman Christians en masse, "I am personally convinced about you that you yourselves are full of goodness, having been filled with all knowledge, and are empowered to advise one another" (15:14).

The Structure of Paul's Letter

Salutation. Paul's salutation (1:1–7) is a much expanded version of the normal *sender/recipient/greeting* pattern of Hellenistic letter writing. Paul identifies himself as "a slave of Christ Jesus" and says as such he was called to be an apostle for the gospel. Then he qualifies what he means by "gospel," for it is not just any old "good news"; rather it is that which was promised through the prophets in the scriptures concerning God's Son. At this point Paul introduces what is likely a primitive Christian confessional formula (1:3b–4), for unlike Paul who thinks in terms of the preexistence and divine sonship of the human Jesus, this formula divides the career of the earthly Messiah from his exaltation as the Son of God and moves from one to the other in terms of the resurrection. Notice there is no mention of the cross, the saving significance of Jesus' death, in these lines. The confession is quite likely an expression of the Christology of the Roman church, for Ambrosiaster (see above) continues his remarks about the coming of Christianity to Rome by saying that prior to Paul "the mystery of the cross of Christ had not been set out for them [the Romans] (*non enim expositum illis fuerat mysterium crucis Christi*)."

Paul continues by saying he received grace and the commission of his apostleship from the Lord Jesus Christ in order that the obedience of faith might be brought about among the Gentiles for the sake of Christ's name. In 1:7 Paul addresses the Roman Christians as God's beloved who are called saints. Finally the apostle greets the Roman saints with his characteristic blessing of grace and peace from God and Christ.

Thanksgiving. Paul gives thanks to God for the well-known faith of the Roman Christians. He acknowledges his prayerful desire to visit Rome, but he makes clear that he may do so only in realization of God's will. It is instructive to notice that Paul gives thanks *through* Jesus Christ, so that even his thanksgiving bespeaks the domination of his life by the Lord Jesus Christ whose slave he is. Thus at the outset of the letter a perceptive reader can see that which is of first importance in Romans is not the apostle but the gospel.

The Body of the Letter. In shifting the focus from his thanksgiving to his reason for wanting to visit Rome (1:11), Paul opens the body of the letter. Verses 11–17 of Rom 1 are a prelude to the rest of the body of the letter which falls into three (or four) large parts: 1:18–4:25 (often subdivided into 1:18–3:20 and 3:21–4:25); 5:1–8:39; and 9:1–11:36. In preliminary verses, 1:11–15, the apostle states that he wishes both to strengthen the Roman believers and, therein, to be encouraged himself by them. Then in 1:16–17 he declares the theme of his letter to the Romans. Since these two verses sound the key for all that is played in Romans, we shall focus on them in detail. For clarity they appear here in a translation with the subdivisions of the verses marked with letters of the alphabet.

16a   For I am not ashamed of the gospel,

16b   for it is the power of God unto the salvation of all who believe:

16c   both to the Jew first and also to the Greek.

17a   For the righteousness of God is being revealed in it from faith unto faith

17b   exactly as it has been written,

17c   "The one who by faith is righteous will live."

Paul speaks here of *the righteousness of God* as being revealed in the gospel (17a), and he defines the gospel per se as "the power of God unto the salvation of all who believe" (16b). Thus Paul understands that the power of God brings about salvation and that God's righteousness is revealed in the power. A relationship exists, therefore, between the righteousness of God and salvation, for both are "being revealed" or are results of the power of God. The nature of this relationship becomes clear when one considers the meaning of the ambiguous phrase "from faith unto faith" (Greek: *ek pisteōs eis pistin*) in v. 17a. For Paul the prepositions, "from" and "unto," often connote apocalyptic realms of power. Thus, here, Paul says that out of the faithfulness of God the faith of humanity is brought into existence. Paul's apocalyptic thought patterns show here in his saying that faith itself comes as a key portion of the salvation that God's saving power effects. Indeed Paul names faith (believing) as the characteristic of those who experience the salvation which is brought about by the power of God (16b), and so the two phrases may be viewed in direct relation to one another:

> the power of God   unto   *salvation* (16b)

and

> *from faith*   unto   *faith* (17a)

Relating these phrases in this manner allows one to see that both phrases depict a motion that is revelatory in nature. Moreover one learns that God's faithfulness, shown in God's power, creates salvation, shown in the faith of humanity.

From this starting point Paul ponders, in the rest of the body of the letter, God's powerful righteousness and its meaning for humanity. In 1:18–3:20 the apostle describes the depraved condition of humanity that necessitated the revelation of God's powerful, saving righteousness. In fine Paul exposes the sinful guilt of the Gentiles by cataloging (1:18–32), in the style of Jewish apologetics, the shameful practices of the Gentiles. While not all Gentiles stooped to what Paul describes as the depths of wickedness, even those who do not are guilty of having tolerated such behavior in others (1:32). Thus no Gentile escapes guilt. Next (2:1–3:20) Paul turns to the Jews, whom he describes as relying upon the law and Jewish observances for their salvation. Yet Paul says they do not keep the law (2:23), but even if they did the workings of the law will not set any human in right standing with God. To sum up: Paul says in 1:18–3:20 that "both Jews and Gentiles alike are under sin" (3:9)—no one from the best to the worst of humanity escapes this assessment. One should understand that Paul is not ranking human sins; instead he is illustrating general human sinfulness. Anyone concerned to use one or more of these verses in order to prove how sinful someone else is has not grasped Paul's point: *all humanity stands equally guilty of sin before God!*

The following major section of the letter, 3:21–4:25, announces and argues that the righteousness of God (God's saving power) has been revealed in the faith of Jesus Christ (Jesus' faith), so that now God's saving power operates in the creation of faith among believers (3:21–26). Moreover, since faith comes from God, the person of faith (the believer) has nothing of which to boast (3:27). The remainder of this section marshals arguments from Old Testament scriptures (primarily focused on the Abraham story) that one is saved by faith. Only as God through Christ creates and sustains faith in the believer is he or she saved by *grace*, whereas those depending upon the law place their full trust in their own failing (failed!) efforts to satisfy God. The good news Paul proclaims is that as God raised Jesus from the dead, so also God raises up faith in those in need of being set right with God (4:23–25).

Having declared that God's gracious power creates saving faith, Paul explicates the concrete meaning of the "good news" in 5:1–8:39. He first expounds upon what humanity is freed *from*: the power of death (5:1–21); the power of sin (6:1–23); and the power of the law (7:1–25). Then the apostle focuses on what humanity is freed *for*: life in the Spirit (8:1–39). Paul's arguments in this portion of the letter run deeply, and they are not immediately clear to modern readers unfamiliar with the style of Jewish apologetics. But, in general Paul explores the reality of Christian freedom by contrasting the *old* with the *new*: Adam with Christ (5:12–21), life in sin before baptism with life in grace after baptism (6:1–14), enslavement to sin leading to death with enslavement to obedience leading to eternal life (6:15–23), and life under the law with life in the Spirit (7:1–6).

Apart from these contrasts, however, Paul ponders Christian life. First, in 5:1–11 he examines the peace with God that Christians have which allows them to live rejoicing despite the paradoxical nature of earthly existence. Later, 7:7–25 is an excursus on the impotence of the law and the impotence of humanity to achieve salvation. Indeed in tandem the law and humanity fell victim to the deceitful power of sin and thereby humanity is left in the lurch, in need of rescue. Having exposed this horrible plight Paul announces that thanks to God humanity has been rescued by the Lord Jesus Christ. Finally, in Rom 8 Paul offers his most extensive treatment of the nature of Christian life. He states that Christians live in the powerful sphere of God's Spirit, as God's children, hoping for the full form of salvation that will be God's (and thus the Christians') triumph over all evil opposition.

The last major section of the body of the letter, chapters 9–11, takes up the problem of Israel's unbelief. Much is made of these chapters. Elaborate and precise (though often different) positions are developed from Rom 9–11 on the so-called doctrine of *predestination*. Usually the argument goes that God determined in advance that some would be saved and others would be damned. If one objects that God is unjustly arbitrary in so acting, Rom 9:10–24 is called up in defense of the Creator's right to do with creation whatever suits divine pleasure. Often, to save face for God and in defense of "freedom of the (human) will," some argue that God merely *knows* in advance what course human lives will take; thus "predestination" is taken to mean only God's permissive foreknowledge.

A red flag needs to be raised regarding both interpretations (and other similar ones), for they are not fair to the text of Romans. In the first place Rom 9–11 is not a timeless observation about divine predestination or foreknowledge. Paul writes, troubled by and struggling with the general failure of Jews to believe that Jesus is the Christ. Rather than formulating abstract timeless truth Paul labors to explain a historical reality. He does so with an absolute conviction that God is God, that God the Creator is capable of ruling over creation, and that "the word of God has not failed" (9:6). Thus Paul attributes what he sees happening in the world around him to the powerful, mysterious activity of God. He claims that God creates both belief and unbelief— that God gives some faith and hardens the hearts of others. Moreover God does all this for a purpose. Follow what Paul says about Israel and the Gentiles:

"[God] has mercy on whomever he wills and hardens whomever he wills" (9:18).

"Has God rejected his people? Certainly not!" (11:1).

"In the present time there is a remnant from the call of grace" (11:5).

"Did they stumble so they may fall? Certainly not! But by their trespass salvation comes to the Gentiles so as to make them jealous" (11:11).

"Notice then God's kindness and severity" (11:22).

"Brethren, I want you to understand this mystery . . . a hardening has come upon part of Israel until the full number of the Gentiles may come in and thus all Israel will be saved" (11:25–26).

"For in the same way that you [Gentiles] were once disobedient to God but now have experienced mercy through their
[Israel's] disobedience, thus also they now have been disobedient because of the mercy given to you in order that
they may receive mercy" (11:30–31).

"For God consigned all people to disobedience in order that
he may have mercy on all" (11:32).

The outcome of this brief survey of Rom 9–11 shows that the God
Paul believes in and whose activity he describes is even odder than
most predestinarians realize. God does act arbitrarily with the authority
of the Creator over creation and presently God's wrath is upon some
while his mercy touches others; but this situation exists because, in
doing what he is doing, God is moving toward a goal, namely, *to
have mercy on all humanity!* If God's method, as described by Paul,
seems odd, one should take comfort in Paul's having referred to what
God is up to as a *mystery.*

To sum up. Israel's condition of unbelief is not a permanent state.
It is the result of God's working, using Israel as his tool in the extension of mercy to all humanity. In other words, God hardened part
of Israel to save all the Gentiles so that ultimately all Israel will be
saved.

Parenesis. In Romans Paul offers his single largest set of observations and practical instructions on Christian life. Rom 12:1–8 sets
the tone for everything that follows through 15:13, for in these eight
verses Paul says the Christian is to live giving himself or herself wholly
to God's will. Christians are not to focus on their privileged status
but upon their opportunities for service.

After a string of practical admonitions (12:9–21) Paul exhorts the
Romans to give the governing authorities their rightful respect (13:1–
8). He bases his argument on natural law, as did other Jewish thinkers
of the time. Thus Paul assumes that even the fallen world can *point*
to God, for God is the giver of order. Here, again, the apostle's statements are not systematic metaphysical theory, but a temporally qualified pastoral directive.

In 13:11–14 Paul posits eschatology as the motivation for Christian living. Because the time is what it is and because the end is near,

Christians know to live out-of-sync with the standards of a benighted, self-centered world.

Following such general admonitions, 14:1–15:13 takes up the specific question of "the strong" and "the weak" in the Roman church. Who are these groups? What is the evidence? Nothing in Romans suggests that the strong and the weak are factions like those in Corinth. Moreover in Rom 15:1 Paul clearly stands with the strong, whereas in the Corinthian correspondences Paul adamantly declared his *weakness*. Rom 14:1 offers a key. There Paul writes of "the weak of faith." Apparently these are Christians whose faith has not relieved them of doubts concerning some elements of Christian freedom, and their scruples cause friction in the community. In dealing with this problem Paul addresses the strong. He instructs them not to judge their more scrupulous co-religionists and, more importantly, not to do anything to antagonize them. Paul says the selfless, sacrificial service of Christ himself is the model of Christian relations.

Closing. The conclusion to Romans is different from that of any other Pauline letter. It falls into three sections. First, Paul briefly describes the guidelines of his own missionary activity (Rom 15:14–21). Second, he explains why he wishes to come to Rome after he completes his work in the eastern Mediterranean by taking the collection to Jerusalem (15:22–29). In conjunction with his travel plans Paul asks for the support of the Romans in prayer (15:30–31). Third, the apostle appends a note commending Phoebe to the church in Rome and sending his greetings to all his friends and acquaintances there (16:1–23).

Paul's Message to the Romans

In his letter to Rome Paul desires to lay out his gospel and its relevance for the believers in Rome. In doing this Paul takes up familiar themes that appeared in past letters—especially the law and Christ, Abraham, Adam and Christ, baptism, Christian service, and Christian relations. But he neither merely summarizes nor abstracts his earlier thinking. He directs a message he believes to be inherently powerful to a church he plans to visit. As his letters were used in previous controversies as an extension of his presence or apostleship, so now Paul surely envisaged that his letter to Rome would stand in his stead and edify the believers among whom he planned to labor soon.

Paul's letter is an introduction of himself and his message. Perhaps it is intended to assuage reservations, but certainly he aimed at promoting harmony and, thereby, at insuring a good reception for his ministry.

Theological Keys to Romans

Essentially Paul proclaims the gospel and ramifications of God's work in *the Christ-event*, which we may think of as *a divine light*:

1. It shines on humanity, revealing the need for God's righteousness (Rom 1:18–3:20).

2. It is a beacon of God's revealed righteousness or saving power (Rom 3:21–4:25).

3. It forms a beam that illuminates the way of Christian freedom created and revealed by God (Rom 5:1–8:39).

4. It reveals a crisis concerning Israel (Rom 9:1–11:36).

5. It signals God's will for the Christian community (Rom 12:1–15:13).

BIBLIOGRAPHY

C. K. Barrett, *A Commentary on the Epistle to the Romans* (HNTC; New York: Harper & Row, 1957).

K. Barth, *The Epistle to the Romans* (6th ed.; Oxford: University Press, 1933).

R. E. Brown and J. P. Meier, *Antioch and Rome* (New York: Paulist, 1983).

C. E. B. Cranfield, *A Critical and Exegetical Commentary on the Epistle to the Romans,* 2 vols. (ICC; Edinburgh: Clark, 1975).

C. H. Dodd, *The Epistle of Paul to the Romans* (MNTC; New York: Harper, 1932).

K. P. Donfried, ed., *The Romans Debate* (Minneapolis: Augsburg, 1977).

E. Käsemann, *Commentary on Romans* (Grand Rapids: Eerdmans, 1980).

M. Luther, *Commentary on the Epistle to the Romans, 1515–1516* (published 1552—English translation 1954).

J. A. T. Robinson, *Wrestling with Romans* (Philadelphia: Westminster, 1979).

Philippians

The church in Philippi was the first one Paul founded on European soil. Paul maintained a positive relationship with the Philippian congregation throughout his ministry—and so far as can be determined it was only in his relationship with Philippi that the apostle broke his custom of not accepting money from those to whom he preached and among whom he ministered.

Paul's Relationship to the Philippians

The story of Paul's first encounter with the Philippians is told in Acts 16. In response to a vision (16:9) Paul and his cohorts went from Asia Minor to proclaim the gospel in Macedonia (16:11). They sailed from Troas in Asia Minor to the European port city Neapolis which was eight miles from Philippi. Acts 16:12 says that the missionary band arrived in Philippi "which is the foremost city of the region of Macedonia, a colony." The Greek text is uncertain here, and it is indeed difficult to understand what Luke meant by calling Philippi "the leading city" of Macedonia, for Thessalonica was the capital of the region. Regardless of what "leading/foremost" (Greek: *prōtos*) means, Luke does communicate something about Philippi's noteworthy history when he records that the city was a "colony" (RSV over-translates here = "Roman colony" which is accurate historically but is not what the text says). Philippi was built by and named for Philip of Macedonia, the father of Alexander the Great, in 358/357 B.C. In 31 B.C. Octavian (Caesar Augustus) made Philippi a Roman military colony. The city was, therefore, an important one with a largely Latin population and with legal privileges to match.

Whatever Luke meant by his description of the city, one learns that the missionaries stayed in Philippi some days and then on a sabbath went outside the city gate to a spot where some God-fearing women had assembled. The first convert was a business woman, Lydia, who along with her household became hostess to the preaching troupe.

It is impossible to determine how long the group remained in Philippi, but as a result of an incident concerning a clairvoyant slave girl, Paul and Silvanus ended up in prison. (Notice, the charge against Paul and Silvanus was that they were Jews, disturbing the city, advocating unlawful customs!) While the two were imprisoned miraculous events occurred and the town jailer was converted, with his household. Later Paul and Silvanus were vindicated, yet they complied with the request of the city magistrates that they leave Philippi.

With certainty one can know that Paul visited Philippi once after his initial ministry there, for Acts 20:6 mentions a departure from Philippi. One may speculate, however, with some security that Paul visited Philippi one or two other times. From the fall of A.D. 52 to the spring of 55 Paul labored in Ephesus. In 2 Cor 2:13; 7:5 one reads that while he was residing in Ephesus Paul temporarily traveled to Macedonia to meet Titus in order to learn of the outcome of Titus' trip to Corinth in his behalf (see above). Perhaps he visited Philippi at this time. Later, at the conclusion of his Ephesian residence (Acts 19:1–20:2), the apostle traveled via Macedonia to Corinth where he spent the winter of A.D. 55–56 before taking the collection to Jerusalem. Paul may well have visited Philippi as he moved from Ephesus through Macedonia to Corinth, for as Acts 20:2 says, Paul went through Macedonia giving the believers there much encouragement prior to going to Greece. After the winter in Corinth Paul set out for Jerusalem, but he traveled somewhat circuitously, going again through Macedonia. Here Acts 20:6 mentions Philippi specifically.

Scholars debate the question of Paul's location at the time he wrote to Philippi. It is only certain that Paul was in jail when he wrote; thus three locations are suggested: Ephesus, Caesarea, and Rome. The Ephesian imprisonment is a scholarly hypothesis that seeks to make sense of Paul's long stay in Ephesus and the mention of opposition (1 Cor 16:8–9), affliction, and peril (1 Cor 15:32; 2 Cor 1:8–10) in that city. But it is best not to ascribe Philippians to an Ephesian imprisonment; for there is no mention of such an incarceration in either Paul's letters or Acts, and the failure to mention the collection differentiates this letter from the others (Galatians, 1 Corinthians, and 2 Corinthians) assigned to Paul's Ephesian residence. Thus, from the known imprisonments, the one mentioned in Philippians could be either in Caesarea or Rome. I prefer Caesarea for three reasons: (1) Paul's consciousness of those who preached Christ from envy or rivalry, out of partisanship, seems most suitable to the milieu of the eastern Mediterranean. (2) The apostle said he plans to visit the Philippians when he was released from prison. We know that Paul planned to go from Jerusalem to Rome and then on to Spain. If he were in Rome it would be odd to backtrack from Rome to Philippi, but if he were in Caesarea it would be natural for him on a trip toward the west to travel by land through Macedonia. (3) The hope Paul expressed concerning his release would be natural when he, as a prisoner, learned that Festus was to replace Felix; but it is not clear that anyone facing Nero would be optimistic. This issue may never be resolved, but whatever Paul's exact location at the time of writing, his letter to the Philippian church reveals that he viewed this community of Christians with warm affection and high regards.

The Situation That Elicited This Letter

Paul seems to have written this letter for a number of reasons. First, he wrote to thank the Philippians for their gift. This is mentioned explicitly in 4:10–20, but Phil 1:5, 7 may contain veiled reference anticipating the outright thanks at the letter's end. Second, Paul discussed Epaphroditus' visit to him and his imminent return to Philippi. The apostle wished to let the Philippians know the exact situation regarding their messenger and to praise him to his home congregation. Third, Paul addressed problems (or potential problems?) in Philippi.

The Problems in Philippi and
the Thinking That Accompanied Them

Clearly there was some affliction of the Philippian Christians from without the church (1:28–30), but this seems to be a continuation of the same, or same kind of, opposition that Paul and Silvanus originally faced, that is, opposition from local non-Jews. There is no reason to understand that this problem was related to the internal life of the congregation.

There was, however, an internal problem about which Paul wrote—namely, a disagreement between two women, Euodia and Syntache. Having labored with one another and with others in the gospel ministry, they were at odds at the time of Paul's writing. The exact nature of their difference cannot be determined from Philippians, but their failure to be like-minded concerned Paul.

Further there is Paul's statement at 3:2 (often labeled an "outburst") warning of outside interlopers. Scholars debate whether Paul was attacking Jewish, Jewish Christian, or "gnosticizing" missionaries. From what is said in Philippians there is no reason that Paul's warning must apply to a specific situation, for if there were specific individuals here, whom Paul was opposing, he surely would have reacted in a sharper fashion. Paul's reference to "dogs" may strike the twentieth century reader as harsh language, but it was the very title claimed by every Cynic street philosopher-preacher (Greek, *kyōn* = literally "dog" = "Cynic") and was not so offensive in Paul's own context. Moreover, Paul's statement, "Look out!" (Greek: *blepete*) is not necessarily an outburst. Indeed, it could mean as little as "regard" (that is, "consider"), but, in any case, from the text it is not clear that Paul is in a lather. Paul seems here to be issuing a generic warning against all systemic human righteousness which can give practitioners an artificial sense of self-perfection.

The Structure of Paul's Letter

The study of Philippians has led scholars to a variety of understandings of the structure of this letter. Like 2 Corinthians this letter is the subject of various partition theories. Scholars frequently find in this one letter fragments of other earlier letters that were later joined by an editor to produce canonical Philippians.

Those holding partition theories usually subscribe to one of two basic hypotheses. First, some older scholars divided Philippians into two parts 1:1–3:1 and 3:2–23. (Neither original letter necessarily survives intact.) This reading of Philippians has essentially lost support among current scholars. Rather, now, scholars who understand Philippians to be a composite tend to divide Philippians into three independent letters. One finds slightly different reconstructions of the three "original" letters, but H. Koester is typical of the consensus in holding letter one = 4:10–20, letter two = 1:1–3:1 + 4:4–7 (perhaps + 4:21–23), and letter three = 3:2–4:3 + 4:8–9. The reasons given for making these divisions are (a) the rough transitions from 3:1 to 3:2 and from 4:9 to 4:10, (b) the redundant nature of much of the concluding material in Phil 4, esp. 4:4–7, 9, 20, 21–23, and (c) different situations and concerns reflected in the various parts of the letter.

Despite the impressive argument of this interpretative hypothesis a growing number of scholars are becoming skeptical of viewing Philippians in terms of multiple letters. As we saw above, Paul does have different motivations for writing this letter, and he speaks here of one thing and there of another. But the letter coheres linguistically and thematically. Throughout the letter Paul directs the Philippians to "rejoice" (1:18, 19; 2:28; 3:1; 4:4 [two times], 10). Moreover, throughout the letter Paul holds up to the Philippians certain models of selfless, sacrificial service: Christ (2:5–11), Timothy (2:20–22), Epaphroditus (2:25–30), and Paul (3:17). The following analysis recognizes Paul's shifting concerns but studies the letter as a unified communication, for the shifts in thought and expression are neither illogical nor impossible and the language and themes of the letter seem homogenous.

PHILIPPIANS	
Salutation	1:1–2
Thanksgiving	1:3–11
Body of the Letter	1:12–3:21
Parenesis	4:1–9
Closing	4:10–23

Salutation. The opening of the letter is brief (1:1–2), but these lines raise matters of significance that are discussed extensively. One learns that Paul and Timothy are the authors and that they identify themselves as "slaves of Christ Jesus" (compare Romans 1:1). This designation probably indicates there is no attack in Philippi against Paul's gospel or ministry (compare Gal 1:1; 1 Cor 1:1; 2 Cor 1:1).

Moreover, notice that these "slaves" of Christ Jesus greet the "holy ones in Christ Jesus who are in Philippi with the overseers and ministers." The location of these Christians "in Christ Jesus" takes precedence over their geographical position. Indeed it is the location "in Christ" that makes "holy ones" or "saints" of the Philippians.

The mention in the greeting of "the overseers and ministers" is unique in the Pauline corpus and has sparked much discussion. The RSV causes serious problems by translating "bishops and deacons." Modern readers immediately and anachronistically retroject later church offices into the Pauline period. But the absence of other such mentions of "overseers and ministers" in Paul's greetings should warn against this. In short, from the evidence in Paul's letters, the best understanding of this greeting is that offered by J.-F. Collange. Collange takes the Greek words in apposition to one another, so that "overseers and ministers" refers to the same people. Thus "overseers" refers to the leaders of the congregation and "ministers" refers to the activity of these leaders. In other words, there is no position without service in a Pauline congregation.

The greeting is a typical one for Paul's letters. Paul and Timothy issue grace and peace to the Philippians from God and Christ.

Thanksgiving. Phil 1:3–11 forms the thanksgiving. Paul relates that he is thankful in his memory for the Philippians and he expresses this in prayer. Verses 5 and 7 mention Paul's joy at the consistent "partnership" of the Philippians in his ministry and claim they are "shareholders" (Greek: *sygkoinōnous*) with Paul in grace. Likely, these verses are indirect references to the gift(s) of the Philippians to Paul, now in prison, on the mission field. In v. 6 Paul expresses his confidence in the Philippians "up to the day of Jesus Christ," but notice that the cause for his confidence is that God is at work among them. The next verses (vv. 8–11) make clear Paul's love and concern for the Philippian Christians.

The Body of the Letter. Paul immediately takes up the matter of his imprisonment and interprets his situation to the Philippians. He claims things are not as they would appear to a casual observer, for a seemingly negative development (imprisonment) is a positive turn.

Because of his confidence that God works in and through all, especially adversity (!), the apostle can say, "What has happened to me actually has come to advance the gospel!"

Moreover, that the gospel is being preached for a variety of motives does not distress Paul, for the gospel is, in any case, preached. Paul sounds a recurring note when he says he "rejoices" about this preaching. The notion of "rejoicing" becomes a theme of the letter, for Paul uses the verb "to rejoice" (*charein*) and its cognates eleven times and the noun "joy" (*chara*) five times.

Paul rejoices at what has happened to him and about whatever may happen. He explicates his fortune in 1:19–26, saying whatever happens will be for the good, whether life or death. His conviction, however, is that he will be released for the sake of the Philippians— his death would be good primarily for himself and not so much an opportunity for service.

Paul follows his mention of a visit to the Philippians (1:26) with a series of exhortations all of which advocate Christian unity (1:27– 2:18). Paul reminds the Philippians that their own situation(s) in life are opportunities for service to Christ. He holds Christ himself up as the source of encouragement and direction for a Christian life of humble, selfless, sacrificial love. Most scholars understand that in Phil 2:6– 11 Paul incorporates a piece of early Christian liturgical material (a hymn, poem, or antiphonal confession) into the letter. Paul introduces these lines with the admonition, "Have this mind-set which was that of Christ Jesus among yourselves!" This "hymn" focuses on Christ, celebrating the Christ-event in terms of preexistence, incarnation (an act of humility), obedience, death, and resurrection-exaltation. These lofty lines promise that God's work in Christ moves all creation toward cosmic hegemony (vv. 9–11).

Paul does not merely admonish the Philippians to live up to Christ's model; he declares to them that "God is the one working in you both to will and to work out his good desire" (2:13). Once again the apostle thinks of a strange God, one who tinkers even with the human will. Thus nothing is out of bounds in terms of God's activity. With this in mind the Philippians can live in any circumstances, as Paul can live or die, with confidence in God and therefore *rejoicing*.

In 2:19–3:1 Paul lays out the plans he hopes soon to enact. He wants to send Timothy, for he is unselfish and will genuinely care for the Philippians. Furthermore, Paul is going to send Epaphroditus, whom the Philippians earlier sent to Paul as their messenger. Paul highly commends Epaphroditus to his home congregation.

As the exhortations (1:27–2:18) followed Paul's discussion of his situation in 1:12–26, now further directions (warnings and admonitions) in 3:2–21 follow the discussion of Paul's plans (2:19–3:1). First, Paul warns the Philippians to be on guard against those who advocate Jewish observances (the law?). He probably has in mind here the sort of preachers he confronted in Galatians. Thus he delineates his former Jewish credentials (mentioned in Gal 1), all attained under the law, saying that in Christ they are irrelevant, worthless; for now he knows Christ and the Christian hope of resurrection from the dead as a gracious act of God's power.

Paul quickly registers a caveat against the possible misunderstanding that Christians *already* have access to the resurrection glory (3:12–16; compare 1 Corinthians, esp. 1 Cor 15). He warns that attempting to appropriate the resurrection glory in the present has led many astray (as in Corinth).

Parenesis. While much of Philippians (1:27–2:18; 3:2–21) is parenetic in character, in 4:1–9 Paul turns from general teaching and exhortation to specific parenesis for the Philippians. He addresses Euodia and Syntache, pleading with them to come to terms with one another. They should surmise how they are to behave from Paul's comments in the earlier portions of the letter, but Paul calls upon another member of the Philippian congregation to act as an arbitrator. Unfortunately it is not certain whether we know this person's name, for the Greek, *gnēsie syzyge,* can mean "true yokefellow" or name one "loyal Sysygus."

Twice in 4:4 Paul sounds the theme of this letter, saying, "Rejoice!" This returns the letter to a lofty note. In such a key the Philippians are told that in living they are to prefer that which is excellent.

Closing. The end of the letter falls into three parts. Phil 4:10–20 is a full concluding thanksgiving for the support (apparently financial, though obviously tangible) the Philippians have given. Paul insists that part of his apostolic charism is the ability to be sustained by God and thereby to be content in whatever state he is. Nevertheless, he is deeply appreciative for the Philippians' contribution. Final greetings are passed in 4:21–22. Then Paul closes with the grace wish of 4:23.

Paul's Advice to the Philippians

The structure of Paul's letter may be ambiguous and debatable, but his advice is clear. He tells the Philippians to *rejoice in the Lord*. In other words, Paul is convinced that in the sphere of the power of God's salvation the Christians have cause, no matter what the conditions, to rejoice. Moreover, they have ready examples of how they are to live: above all Christ, but also Paul, Timothy, and one of their own, Epaphroditus.

Paul warns against the temptation to perfect oneself, saying that human achievement should be cast aside for Christ. Indeed in comparison to the gain of Christ, all human achievement is sewage (3:8).

Paul directs the Philippians to "stand firm in one Spirit" (1:27), living in a manner worthy of the gospel. This means they will agree with one another (having the same mind as Christ), and they will care for each other (having Christ's humility). Paul's depiction here of the salvation Christians live and look forward to is not so individual as it is cosmic. The apostle declares the cosmic rule of Christ, the crucified one; and in this light he demands that the believers in Philippi live in the same selfless, obedient manner that Christ embodied.

Theological Keys to Philippians

One does well to focus on the "hymn" in Phil 2:6–11. It sketches the career of Christ from his origin in heaven through his death on the cross to his current position as the exalted one. Paul (and the hymn) understands all this to mean that the aim of the Lord is to subdue all creation under the will of the Creator. The vision is that of cosmic hegemony achieved through the career of Christ. The hymn implies the futility of human efforts at righteousness—which only lead to dissension. It shows that God's goal is unity, to be achieved under the rule of Christ; and it makes clear that the source of power for salvation is nothing other than the work of God in Christ.

BIBLIOGRAPHY

F. W. Beare, *The Epistle to the Philippians* (BNTC, 3d ed.; London: Black, 1973).

J.-F. Collange, *The Epistle of Saint Paul to the Philippians* (London: Epworth, 1979—French original 1973).

D. E. Garland, "The Composition and Unity of Philippians. Some Neglected Literary Factors," *NovT* 27 (1985) 141–73.

H. Koester, "Philippians, Letter to the," *IDBSup* 665–66.

J. B. Lightfoot, *St. Paul's Epistle to the Philippians* (4th ed.; London: Macmillan, 1885—reprinted by Hendrickson Publishers, 1981).

Philemon

This brief letter is remarkable among the undisputed letters of Paul, for it is written to an individual. The letter deals with a "personal" problem, the fate of a runaway slave named Onesimus. The letter is not, however, entirely private as is evident from the address: Paul pens the letter with Timothy and greets not only Philemon but also Apphia, Archippus, and the church in Philemon's house. Apparently the apostle anticipated that the letter would be read in the context of the assembled congregation.

Paul's Relationship to
the Church in Philemon's House

The usual approach to Philemon is to read the letter in conjunction with Colossians in order to attain illumination concerning *places* and *date*. Both scholars who do and scholars who do not accept Colossians as an authentic Pauline letter practice such interpretative method. Those who accept Colossians as genuinely Pauline suggest the two letters were written at or about the same time, while those who do not accept Colossians as authentic still use Col 4:9 (the mention of Onesimus) to locate the church in Philemon's house at Colossae.

One should question this line of interpretation. Whether or not Colossians is authentic, Col 4:9 presents a completely different image of Onesimus from that in Philemon. Onesimus is practically introduced in Colossians, for he is called "the faithful and beloved brother, who is one of yourselves." Moreover, he is in a position to address the Colossian congregation in Paul's behalf. This is hardly the status of a returning runaway slave. Furthermore, there is nothing in Philemon per se to suggest Colossae as the destination of the letter. Indeed Paul seems intimately acquainted with the church in Philemon's house (v. 22), and so the congregation could be any one of several—but it is not likely in Colossae, for according to Col 1:3–8 Paul did not found and did not know that church personally. Thus the question of which church Paul is addressing is open, and the question of Paul's relationship to that church cannot be described historically. Yet Philemon itself yields some data: Verse 19 makes clear that Philemon was converted by Paul and vv. 4–5, 22 imply that some relationship was maintained between Paul and Philemon.

Furthermore, one cannot with certainty locate Paul at the time of the writing of this letter. From the letter one learns he was in prison (vv. 1, 9–10, 13) and that he planned to visit Philemon when he was released (v. 22). In addition, there is no mention of the collection in this letter. Thus it may be that the letter comes from the same time of imprisonment in Caesarea as did Philippians. But this is a best guess, not a definite conclusion, for good cases can be made for Paul's being in either Ephesus or Rome.

The Problem or Situation Eliciting the Letter

Onesimus, a slave who belonged to Philemon, fled from his master. He made his way to Paul; one cannot determine how or why or even if he did so deliberately. Nevertheless, Onesimus was converted by Paul, and subsequently he was helpful to Paul. Indeed after Onesimus' conversion a close relationship had developed between the apostle and this fugitive slave. But at the time of the writing of this letter Paul was returning Onesimus to his master, in strict compliance with Roman law concerning runaway slaves. In this letter Paul intercedes with Philemon in Onesimus' behalf.

The letter is not concerned with "opponents" or with any "problem" in the usual sense of the other letters. The most intense debate about this letter arises from our later sensibilities, namely, why did not Paul explicitly oppose slavery as un-Christian?

The Structure of Paul's Letter

In pondering Paul's work as an apostle we examined the structure of Philemon in relation to the form of standard Hellenistic letters. This letter conforms nicely to the expected format of a first century letter, but we noted a few "changes" that set Paul's letters apart from normal secular letters. In considering this letter in more detail we will see how rich a communication this deceptively simple seeming letter is.

PHILEMON	
Salutation	1–3
Thanksgiving	4–7
Body of the Letter	8–21
Parenesis	22
Closing	23–25

Salutation. Paul names his "brother" Timothy as the co-author of the letter, but he refers to himself only as "a prisoner *of* Christ Jesus." Translations that render this self-designation "a prisoner *for* Christ Jesus" fail to catch the subtlety of the statement; Paul claims here that though he is in captivity he is truly the captive not of governmental authorities but of the Lord. Thus the final control over his life rests with God, not humans. Paul does not claim the title of apostle and refrains from exercising such authority in this communication. Indeed he addresses Philemon as an equal, calling him a "fellow-worker."

In writing to his "equal" Paul does not issue an order, and he does not make a request. Rather he recommends to Philemon what he can do.

Thanskgiving. Paul informs Philemon that he has him in his prayers and that praying he thanks God for Philemon and the love and faith which he (Philemon) manifests. Paul says he has great joy and comfort from Philemon's love *because he (Philemon) refreshes the hearts of the saints.*

The Body of the Letter. Paul makes an appeal for Onesimus. The full force of this appeal is lost to all but the readers of the Greek text, for the body of the letter is full of puns and word plays, the majority of which only function in Greek. In two places Paul forms word plays on the name Onesimus (Greek: *Onēsimos*). This was a common name among slaves that meant "useful." First, Paul puns the meaning of this Greek name in v. 11 when he says that before Onesimus ("Useful") ran away, he was "useless" (Greek: *achrēstos*); but now that Onesimus is a Christian and is returning, he is "really useful" (Greek: *euchrēstos*). Thus Paul says that Onesimus' running away was a turn for the good. Indeed there may be a second level to this play on the meaning of Onesimus' name in the words *useless* (*achrēstos*) and *useful* (*euchrēstos*). The root in both words is *chrēstos* which means "useful" or "serviceable." *Chrēstos* was itself a name frequently given to slaves, but here this stem probably plays on the name or title *Christ* (*christos*). The prefixes *a-* and *eu-* modify the stem (*chrēstos*), *a-* indicating "without" and *eu-* indicating "good" or "well." Thus Paul probably means to imply that prior to being a Christian (i.e., "without Christ" = *a-christos*) Onesimus ("Useful") was "useless" (*achrēstos*), but as a good Christian (*eu-christos*) formerly useless Onesimus is "really useful" (*euchrēstos*).

Second, Paul tells Philemon in v. 20 that he wants some "benefit" (*onaimēn*) from him. While "benefit" and "Onesimus" are not similar in English, *Onēsimos* and *onaimēn* look and sound alike in Greek. Thus using paronomasia Paul implies, without saying it, that he desires Onesimus from Philemon.

One other play on words also makes clear what Paul thinks Philemon should do. In v. 7 Paul says "the hearts of the saints have been refreshed through [Philemon]." Then in v. 12 Paul says that Onesimus is his "very heart." Finally in v. 20 Paul declares what "benefit" he desires from Onesimus, namely that he (Philemon) "refresh [Paul's] heart in Christ." Thus Paul calls on Philemon, that Christian heart-refresher, to refresh his (Paul's) heart in Christ, and Paul's heart is none other than Onesimus the slave, himself now "in Christ."

Moreover, in v. 13 Paul tells Philemon what he (Paul) would have done: he would have kept Onesimus; but he leaves it to Philemon to decide what will be done—though Paul certainly dropped enough hints that Philemon would have had a hard time missing the point. Paul demands nothing, but he makes his own preference clear. He adjures Philemon to receive Onesimus "no longer as a slave but more than a slave, as a beloved brother" and to "receive him as me," that is, *as an equal*. Paul says that he is confident of Philemon's "obedience" and that he knows Philemon "will do even more than" he says. Thus without ordering Philemon to do anything, Paul lets him know he should free Onesimus and send him back to Paul.

Paul does not leave the matter here, however. In v. 18 he broaches the legal side of the question. Under Roman law a slave could buy his or her freedom; indeed many did, and on rare occasions some slaves simply were set free. But this was unusual, for slaves were a valuable commodity and normally owners expected some compensation for the loss of the slave's services. Thus under normal circumstances if Onesimus wanted his freedom, it would have cost him; and so, Paul steps in and offers to pay whatever Onesimus might owe. Yet, Paul reminds Philemon that he owes his very self (his salvation?) to the apostle. In short, regarding the cost of Onesimus' freedom, Paul cashes in Philemon's chips!

Parenesis. The letter is replete with gentle, general hortatory material, but Paul issues specific final instructions in v. 22. He tells Philemon he will come to visit as soon as he is out of prison and charges him to prepare a guest room. Imagine Philemon's facing Paul if he did not do what Paul recommended!

Closing. Final greetings are passed to Philemon alone (Greek *se* = "you" singular) from those with Paul. Then Paul pronounces the benediction of the grace of the Lord Jesus Christ upon the whole church in Philemon's house (Greek *hymeis* = "you" plural).

A Theological Key to Paul's "Appeal"

Paul handles the matter of Onesimus' freedom in a businesslike manner. He does not command Philemon to set Onesimus free, nor does he tell him it is the moral thing to do. Instead Paul informs Philemon what he (Paul) would have done, and he expresses his confidence in Philemon to do even more; but he says if a debt is incurred or if a price is involved, it should be charged to his (Paul's) account. Paul's tab, however, already has Philemon's "debt" to the apostle on it, and so there is no real question of payment here. Yet, the logic is that of legally settling a bill, and Paul handles the matter as he docs so that Onesimus is not placed in debt to Philemon for his generosity.

But why did not Paul simply tell Philemon that owning slaves was wrong? Slavery was an accepted social convention in Paul's world. As we have seen Paul had a peculiar view of that world: he thought it was passing away and that soon it would be gone. Therefore he did not attempt to reform society—instead he relativized it, advocating that Christians be primarily concerned with the edification of the church, not their social status. Denouncing slavery was no more a concern of Paul's than was building himself a nice home and founding a Bible college.

BIBLIOGRAPHY

J. B. Lightfoot, *Saint Paul's Epistles to the Colossians and to Philemon* (rev. ed.; London: Macmillan, 1879).

E. Lohse, *Colossians and Philemon* (Hermeneia; Philadelphia: Fortress, 1971).

N. R. Peterson, *Rediscovering Paul: Philemon and the Sociology of Paul's Narrative World* (Philadelphia: Fortress, 1985).

W. G. Rollins, "Philemon, Letter to," *IDBSup* 663–64.

The Letters of the Pauline Heritage

The consideration of the six "disputed" letters of the Pauline corpus comes at this juncture because of the position taken on their authorship in what follows, namely that they are the products of later
students or disciples of Paul. The factors that inform the decisions
about the authorship of these letters are, as will be seen, matters of
language (vocabulary, style, syntax), theology, and the historical sit-
uation(s) presupposed by the letters.

That these letters are included in this book on Paul, even though
they are not regarded as coming from the apostle in this study, results
from these letters forming a portion of the canonical corpus of Pauline
literature that is itself an important part of authoritative Christian scripture. While this study maintains that decisions about authorship are of
primary importance for the study of Paul—his life, letters, and theology—such conclusions about authorship are at most of secondary
importance in the consideration of these letters as scripture. Therefore,
in treating the following letters attention is given to questions of authorship, but that one issue does not dominate the discussion of the
letters. This position reflects a particular understanding of the inspiration of scripture, that the biblical documents are testimony to revelation, not revelation per se. It is striking that those who deny this
understanding of the inspiration of scripture and who defend the Pauline authorship of these six disputed canonical works frequently do
nothing more than defend that Paul wrote these letters; these scholars
too often have very little to say about the content, message, and theological importance of these letters.

Moreover since the Pauline authorship of the six letters that follow is still defended by some responsible critical scholars, the student of the Pauline corpus needs to ponder the message of these canonical letters that claim Paul as their author, whether or not one judges that the apostle produced these works. It may be helpful at this point for the reader to turn to the Appendix for help in understanding the broader issues involved in decisions about the authorship of the disputed letters.

2 Thessalonians

2 Thessalonians is the only book of the New Testament quoted in a national constitution—2 Thess 3:10 is part of the constitution of the U.S.S.R. Independent of this bit of trivia scholars debate the authorship of this letter perhaps more intensely than any other New Testament work, with a slight majority holding the letter to be an authentic Pauline epistle. In what follows we will examine the question of authorship, and after drawing conclusions move on to the content of the letter.

The Question of Authorship

The letter purports to come from Paul with Silvanus and Timothy. Those who accept this claim usually understand that the letter must have been written shortly after 1 Thessalonians, for the letters are remarkably similar in language and form.

Many scholars object, however, to the authenticity of this letter. They cite the close dependence of 2 Thessalonians on 1 Thessalonians and observe striking differences between the letters. For example, about one-third of 2 Thessalonians is exactly the same as 1 Thessalonians; thus demonstrable structural similarities, parallels in vocabulary, and the same themes exist. Yet the letters are different. In tone 1 Thessalonians is warm and loving, but 2 Thessalonians is formal and cool. In addition, 2 Thessalonians has a penchant to moralize (see 2 Thess 3), a tendency that is very unlike Paul. 1 Thess 1:5–7 says the Thessalonian Christians were imitators as they accepted the gospel in affliction and 1 Thess 2:8–9 says Paul worked in service to the gospel as an expression of love; but 2 Thess 3:7–10 says Paul worked to provide an example for the church to imitate. Thus the readers of 2 Thessalonians become imitators by following a demonstrated apostolic work ethic, not by receiving the gospel in affliction; and the dedicated work of the apostle is no longer understood as service to the gospel, but as a moral example against laziness.

Above all those scholars denying Pauline authorship of 2 Thessalonians argue that 1 and 2 Thessalonians are theologically disharmonious. The eschatology of 2 Thess 2:1–12 and that of 1 Thess 4–5 and 1 Cor 15 are not compatible, for if the day of the Lord will come suddenly and unexpectedly like a thief in the night (1 Thessalonians and 1 Corinthians), how can it be preceded and foretold by clear, visible signs (2 Thessalonians)? The question here is not whether Paul could use traditional Jewish apocalyptic images, for he did so in 1 Thess 4–5 and 1 Cor 15; rather the question is whether "signs" are possible for Paul, since he says the end will be completely unexpected. The mixture of statements in 1 Thessalonians and 1 Corinthians on the one hand and 2 Thessalonians on the other seems illogical and contradictory. Indeed 2 Thess 2 does not so much portray an apocalyptic vision of the triumph of God in Christ (see 1 Cor 15 and Phil 2) as it delineates a standard Jewish apocalyptic end-scheme with the stock characters and elements of normal Jewish apocalypses.

Further instances of theological incompatibility are also cited. (1) 1 Thess 1:6–10 treats tribulation as a sign of divine election (as does 2 Corinthians), but 2 Thess 1:4–10 relates tribulation to a scheme of divine reward and retribution. (2) 1 Thess 3:8 calls for a firm standing "in the Lord" but 2 Thess 2:15 calls for a firm standing and holding to the "traditions" that were taught to the Thessalonians.

Finally, many scholars find the emphasis in 2 Thessalonians on the epistle's own authenticity overdone and even obtrusive. For instance 2 Thess 2:2 denies the authenticity of an earlier letter to the Thessalonians, warning against teachings "by letter purporting to be from us." Then 2 Thess 2:5 appeals to the memory of the audience, saying, "Do you not remember when I was still with you . . .?" Ultimately the statement in 2 Thess 3:17 about Paul's handwritten final greeting, calling it "a sign in every [Pauline] epistle," is exaggerated; for several letters, even (especially!) 1 Thessalonians, have no mention of Paul's autograph!

In conclusion, no single argument is sufficiently weighty to demonstrate clearly that 2 Thessalonians was not produced by Paul himself; but the force of the sum of different arguments persuades many scholars that the letter is not an authentic Pauline document. Recognizing the difficulties, some scholars attempt to resolve the problems by holding 2 Thessalonians as an earlier communication than 1 Thessalonians; but this does not work, since it still does not account for the differences between the letters.

For those who understand 2 Thessalonians to be a pseudepigraphical work the question is whether the letter is an *early* or *late* deutero-Pauline writing. If early, then it could be the product of Silvanus and Timothy or someone else writing close to the time of 1 Thessalonians. If late, it could come from an unknown author writing later in the first century (Polycarp is the first to quote 2 Thessalonians in about A.D. 110) using 1 Thessalonians as a model. The latter of these options seem more likely, for 2 Thessalonians seems best to fit a context of persecution late in the first century, when eschatology often led to problems.

The Problem Addressed

From reading 2 Thessalonians one gains quite a different impression of the crisis addressed in Thessalonica from that derived from a reading of 1 Thessalonians. In 1 Thessalonians there was clearly outside persecution that caused the Thessalonians to have doubts and despair. In response to this problem Paul offered eschatological teaching about "the day of the Lord" and exhorted the Thessalonians to encourage one another in light of the assurance they had by knowing of this coming day.

In 2 Thessalonians there is but a vague reference to persecution and it seems abstract when compared to 1 Thess 2:13–16. Rather in 2 Thessalonians there seems to be a crisis related to eschatology that is internal to the church. Specifically *someone has said the day of the Lord has already come* (2:1–2). This line has been swallowed by some and generally has unsettled and alarmed the church.

To put the problem another way, *someone has used eschatological teaching in order to determine daily life*. Notice this is exactly what Paul did in 1 Thessalonians; but there what he said was that eschatology should provide a basis for hope and mutual encouragement.

Whereas Paul said that the day of the Lord "will come," so therefore live in hope, encouraging one another, now someone has said the day of the Lord "has come already." The results of this teaching are seen in the lives of some of the Thessalonian Christians who have put themselves into neutral by quitting work.

Are There Opponents?

Whether or not one posits "opponents" in Thessalonica against whom the remarks of the letter are aimed depends upon how one reads the letter, especially 2:1–12. Some interpreters suggest there are opponents who are described in these verses; these scholars understand the opponents to be outsiders who have brought a new teaching to Thessalonica, like the "opponents" denounced in Galatians and 2 Corinthians.

But the problem here could be similar to that addressed in 1 Corinthians—namely, enthusiastic, immature converts have reached an erroneous conclusion by building upon Paul's own teaching. Indeed there is nothing in 2 Thessalonians that refers to outsiders and there is nothing that clearly identifies "opponents." There are people with a problem, who have wrong-headed ideas and who are in need of correction, but these are not really "opponents."

The Theology of the Problem

Paul's apocalyptic vision of the triumph of God, especially as realized at "the day of the Lord," has been spiritualized so that a new idea has arisen. Some Christians are claiming that the day of the Lord has already come, and for the Christians living on earth this means liberation from all bodily cares. Those holding this belief are idle! Notice, these folks are not waiting for the day of the Lord like so many millenarian cultists, but they are luxuriating in their insight, like so many quasi-gnostics.

The Structure of the Letter

Salutation. The greeting is brief (1:1–2), and is almost exactly the same as that of 1 Thessalonians. The only difference is the addition

---

2 THESSALONIANS

Salutation	1:1–2
Thanksgiving	1:3–12
Body of the Letter	2:1–3:5
Parenesis	3:6–15
Closing	3:16–18

---

of the words "from God the Father and the Lord Jesus Christ" after the greeting of "grace and peace." The additional phrase is Pauline and conforms to Gal 1:3, where God is "the Father" rather than "our Father" as in the rest of Paul's letters.

Thanksgiving. The author offers thanks in 1:3–12. The peculiar element in this section is the reward and retribution scheme articulated in vv. 5–10 (discussed above). This is the only instance of such thought in the letter. Also remarkable is that the salvific reward in store for those Christians who at present suffer is termed "rest" in v. 7. Paul knows and uses the word *anesis* ("rest") in one of his undisputed letters (2 Cor 2:13; 7:5; 8:13), but he uses the word casually, not with theological significance and not in relation to the final salvific state. The thought in 2 Thessalonians is closest to the "rest" motif of Hebrews (see, e.g., Heb 4:3), though there the word for rest is *katapausis*.

The Body of the Letter. The main portion of the letter extends from 2:1 through 3:5 and falls into three parts. 2:1–12 offers a schedule, though without exact temporal references, for the coming of the day of the Lord. First there is "rebellion," and then the "man of lawlessness," "the son of perdition" is revealed. (Those who accept this letter as authentic see this reference as the *first* instance of Christian "anti-Christology." It is striking, however, that 2 Thessalonians names the antichrist as "the son of perdition" and also mentions "the restrainer"; but elsewhere Paul does not even use the title Son of Man for Jesus!) The son of perdition is held back by "the restrainer," a figure like that in Rev 20. This passage goes on to mention the attendant "signs and wonders" of the period of rebellion prior to the end and promises the victory of the Lord Jesus. Notice that this text is consistent with other New Testament apocalyptic eschatological scenes in that there is no hint of *when* the events foretold will come to pass—the mystery remains a mystery; the unknown remains unknown.

A second thanksgiving of sorts comes in 2:13–17. The author explicates the motivation for his thankfulness, namely, because God chose to save the Thessalonians. But the following lines continue by exhorting the readers to stand firm, to hold to the traditions taught them and to be comforted by God in every good work and word (not in the hope of the day of the Lord).

Finally 3:1–5 admonishes the readers to prayerful support for the apostle. Then the author expresses confidence in the readers because of his confidence in God.

Parenesis. Instructions are delivered to the readers in 3:6–15. Of particular concern is the laziness of certain members of the church that probably extends from false eschatological teaching about earthly Christian privileges.

Closing. The letter ends with a pronouncement of "peace" in the presence of the Lord (3:16). Then follows the "autograph" by "Paul." Finally, the benediction of the "grace" of the Lord Jesus Christ is issued to "all" the Thessalonians.

The Solution or Advice

As there are two dimensions to the problem: (1) false eschatological teaching and (2) idleness, so there are two elements to the solution offered. First, the writer denies the particular eschatological teaching and offers a timetable with clear signs for the end. Thus the letter recasts eschatology into the future but gives no assistance for solving the mystery of who these stock apocalyptic figures are. In doing this 2 Thessalonians achieves a second dimension of the solution: a wedge is driven between eschatological teaching and present Christian activity or life. In other words eschatology is not shown to be the basis of hope and encouragement. It is an unsolvable mystery, an insoluble lump, not to be entertained. Rather than focusing on the future and engaging in eschatological speculation the Thessalonians are called to imitate the work ethic of the apostle Paul

A Theological Key to 2 Thessalonians

One gains interpretative entry into the text by recognizing the relationship between eschatology and daily Christian life in both 1 and 2 Thessalonians. In 1 Thessalonians eschatology and life are bonded. From eschatology Christians gain hope and are strengthened to give mutual encouragement. In 2 Thessalonians eschatology and life are rent asunder. Eschatology is offered and affirmed, but it is rendered essentially irrelevant as a future mystery. The end (and the mysterious events before it) is something to be anticipated, but daily life is determined by imitation of the zealous labor of the apostle and comfort is derived from "every good work" (3:17).

BIBLIOGRAPHY

E. Best, *A Commentary on The First and Second Epistles to the Thessalonians* (BNTC; London: Black, 1972).

K. P. Donfried, "The Cults of Thessalonica and the Thessalonian Correspondence," *NTS* 31 (1985) 336–56.

I. H. Marshall, *1 and 2 Thessalonians* (NCB; Grand Rapids: Eerdmans, 1983).

Colossians

Colossae is the least important city in which there was a church to which one of the thirteen "Pauline" letters is addressed. The city was located in the Lycus River Valley in the southern part of the province of Phrygia. It lay alongside a major trade route that ran from Ephesus in the west to Miletus in the east. Today this area is western Turkey.

Colossae once had been a leading city of the region, a center of the wool industry where residents engaged in textile weaving, dyeing, and sales. But by the mid-to-late first century Colossae's neighbor cities, Laodicea (about ten miles away) and Hierapolis (about twelve and a half miles distant) were more significant than Colossae which had become an insignificant market town.

In the mid-first century the population of Colossae was an indigenous one made up of Phrygians along with Greeks and Jews who had settled there several generations earlier. The Jewish population of the region was sizeable, for a statement by Cicero (*Pro Flacco* 28.68) is interpreted to indicate that in Laodicea alone the Jewish male population was between ten and eleven thousand.

Religiously the area was highly syncretistic. For example, the cult of Cybele flourished (some scholars understand Col 2:11, 23 in relation to the practices of this cult). Isis and Apollo were also revered in this region, as were many other popular gods. In addition the influence of eastern religion, particularly the Iranian types, was felt in the area. Even the Judaism of the Lycus River Valley was a typical cultural mix of first century Hellenism—that is, it blended itself with the ascetic rigorism of the Phrygian Cybele cult, with elements of Iranian religion as known from Mithraism, and with wisdom teaching and speculation as exemplified by Isis and Apollo mystery cults.

In A.D. 61 an earthquake struck the Lycus Valley, apparently destroying Colossae and its neighboring cities. Laodicea was rebuilt and prospered, but nothing more is ever heard of Colossae. Thus scholars often regard A.D. 61 as the *terminus ad quem* for the writing of this letter. But this position is debated and depends in large part on the question of authorship, for if the letter does not come from the pen of the apostle Paul (the conclusion of many scholars) there is no need for the letter to serve the community it claims to address.

Paul's Relationship to the Church
at Colossae and the Question of Authorship

The letter says it was borne to the Colossians by Tychicus and Onesimus (the slave from Philemon?), and according to the letter Paul had never visited the church at Colossae (2:1). Rather the Colossians "learned" the gospel from Epaphras, a beloved fellow-servant with Paul (1:3–8). Col 4:12 seems to mean that Epaphras was a native of Colossae, or at least of the Lycus Valley area.

If the letter is genuinely Pauline it clearly comes from the apostle who is in prison, though the exact location is not stated. It is not necessary to lump this letter together with Philemon and Philippians, however. We saw above that in Colossians Onesimus is not likely a returning slave, for he has sufficient status to be Paul's agent and it is even necessary to introduce or describe him to the readers (oddly the same is true of Epaphras at 4:12–13). Indeed the universally recognized differences in the levels of theological expression in these letters (Colossians seems more "developed" than the letters previously studied) suggest it is prudent to separate Colossians from Philemon and Philippians temporally. For those who accept the Pauline authorship of Colossians this may be done by assigning Colossians to the time of Paul's imprisonment in Rome.

Other scholars separate Colossians from Philemon and Philippians in more than temporal terms; they deny that the letter is an authentic Pauline communication. R. E. Brown estimates that about sixty percent of critical scholars judge that the apostle did not write this letter. Why?

The *vocabulary* of Colossians is remarkably different from that in the undisputed letters of Paul. Forty-eight words are found only in Colossians among Paul's letters, and thirty-three of these words are *hapax legomena* (they occur only one time in the whole New Testament). While many of the odd words are used in relation to the problem being addressed by the letter and may thereby be accounted for in light of the particularity of the situation, still the percentage of unusual words is extraordinarily high.

The *style* of the letter is strikingly different from Paul's manner of writing in his other letters. Even in English translation this letter is stylistically different from the undisputed letters. Colossians contains long sequences of genitives in constructions like that at 1:13, "the kingdom of the Son of his love." There are redundant combinations of parallel terms like "praying and petitioning" (1:9). Many of the sentences are long and obfuscating—for instance, in Greek 1:9–20 is a single sentence!

The *theology* of Colossians is distinct from the letters we have previously examined. Scholars acknowledge this difference whether they argue for or against Pauline authorship, claiming that Colossians shows a marked development in Paul's Christology and ecclesiology. To illustrate these differences:

(1) Col 1:13 refers to the kingdom of the Son, whereas elsewhere Paul always writes of the kingdom as being God's. This is but one instance that illustrates the elaborate Christology of the letter. The tendency toward a lofty Christology permeates the letter, so that in general Christ is not the revelation of the power of God (in weakness); rather he is he "in whom all the treasures of wisdom and knowledge are hidden" (2:3). In fact, Colossians regards Christ in so absolute a fashion that he is that which the Colossians have received (2:6); whereas, by contrast, in all other Pauline letters Paul says he and other Christians received (*paralambanein*) the gospel, traditional teaching material, or the word of God.

(2) Col 1:18 and 2:19 portray Christ as the "head" of his body which is the Church. This notion is striking in two ways. First, in his undisputed letters Paul uses the word *church* (*ekklēsia*) frequently, and most often in reference to local communities of Christians; but here

the usage is absolute, referring to *the Church* comprehensively and indicating all Christians everywhere (hereafter the capitalization of *C* indicates this universal notion). Indeed in Colossians *Church* is used in so universal a fashion that it indicates more than an earthly entity, for it affects the heavenly powers! Second, in 1 Cor 12 and Rom 12 Paul uses the "body" ("of Christ" in 1 Cor 12) as a metaphor for discussing the charisms of the individual Christians in the larger congregation. He does this to explain how these gifts are complementary "parts" of one united whole. Yet from Paul's concept of a "body" of Christians that labors and suffers "as one," Colossians moves the body imagery to the level of a corporate entity *with Christ himself as the Head or Lord over the body.* Thus the body itself is no longer *identified with Christ* as in Romans and 1 Corinthians, but it is *joined to Christ* who is its head.

(3) Col 1:24 says Paul suffers for the Church, not for the gospel (as in 1 Thess 2 or Phil 1:12). Moreover Colossians says Paul's sufferings complete that which is *lacking in Christ's afflictions for the sake of his body, the Church.* This shift in focus from the gospel to the Church is striking, but the idea that something was lacking with regard to Christ's own afflictions is, in the opinion of many scholars (myself included), utterly irreconcilable to the mind of Paul who understands himself as "an imitator," not "a fulfiller" of Christ.

(4) Col 1:25 says Paul is a minister of the Church, not an apostle of Christ Jesus, nor a minister of a new covenant (2 Cor 3:6), nor a minister of God (2 Cor 6:4). In Paul's undisputed letters the apostle envisions himself as a servant of God and thinks that God's power works through himself as God's servant in forming the new covenantal community; but in Colossians the Church is somehow that which Paul is serving. This idea relates to (and explains?) how "Paul" fulfills Christ's afflictions for the Church in Col 1:24.

(5) Col 1:24–26 says that *Paul* reveals the mystery (of God) hidden through the ages. In 1 Cor 2:6–16, however, Paul says *the Spirit* reveals the secret of God. Perhaps in 1 Corinthians Paul did mean that the Spirit revealed the mystery through his apostolic work, but it is remarkable that in a Pauline epistle, at this point, there is no reference to the Spirit. Indeed in Colossians there is only one innocuous mention of the Spirit (see Col 1:8).

(6) Col 2:12 and 3:1 say that in baptism the Christian dies *and*

rises with Christ, whereas elsewhere (see esp. 1 Cor 15 and Rom 6) Paul consciously and conscientiously guards against saying that the Christian is already experiencing the resurrection power of Christ.

(7) Many scholars find Col 2:17 a particularly problematic statement to attribute to Paul. The verse follows 2:16, which is clearly a discussion of elements of the law, for sabbath is specifically mentioned. Col 2:17 then says these portions of the law are "only a shadow of that to come, whereas the body is of Christ." The contrast between shadow and body builds on Platonic philosophy, understanding the shadow as a mere appearance of the reality, here = the body. Though the law is associated here with "the elements of the cosmos" (*ta stoicheia tou kosmou*) as in Gal 4:9 (see Col 2:8, 20), this is not Paul's usual manner of thinking about the law. Here there is continuity, and the law is merely inferior to Christ who is understood to realize the law. Here there is no conflict between the law and Christ; they are compatible, though Christ is superior. Here Christ is not cursed by the law (Gal 3:13) and the law is not put to an end by Christ (Rom 10:4).

Conclusion. Even noticing many or all the points examined above, many critical scholars argue that only Paul could produce a letter so Pauline and yet with such clear development. They argue that a "forger" would surely have done a better job, as did whoever produced Paul's letter to the Laodiceans (see the Appendix). A few scholars, like E. Schweizer, take Timothy's co-authorship of Colossians seriously and argue that Timothy was the primary author of this letter. This accounts for the theological developments and the tendency of the letter to dwell upon the apostle (e.g., 1:24–26). But a slight majority of New Testament scholars (including myself) assess the significance of the differences between Colossians and the undisputed letters to imply that Paul neither wrote this letter nor had a hand in its production; rather it is a product of another anonymous first century Christian who wrote in Paul's name. Therefore in what follows, *Colossians* refers to the original readers of the letter but does not assume that these people were living in Colossae, which may have been already destroyed.

The Problem or Situation Eliciting the Letter

The Colossians have been or are in danger of being enamored of an ascetic, syncretistic philosophy. Col 2:8 mentions a "philosophy" based on "human tradition" that is being presented. That this philosophy was ascetic in its orientation seems clear from the mention of circumcision (2:11) and the references to dietary restrictions and calendar observation (2:16, 21[?]). Indeed 2:23 refers to rigorous devotion, self-abasement, and severe treatment of the body.

Thus far the author of Colossians could be denying a "philosophy" that is no more than an ascetic form of Judaism, but other information in Colossians suggests that an unusual syncretistic form of religion is being opposed. Col 2:18 indicates that self-abasement is somehow tied to "the worship of angels." Scholars are in general agreement on this much about Colossians, but beyond this there is lively debate; for the phrase (Greek: *thrēskeia tōn angelōn*) is ambiguous and can mean either (1) the angels are being worshiped or (2) the worshiping that the angels do. The mention of visions that puff one up that immediately follows this phrase probably indicates that the Colossians are not revering the angels as the objects of worship, but are intent upon worshiping with the angels. Thus the self-abasing asceticism in which the Colossians engage is a way of qualifying themselves to participate with the angels in extraterrestrial worship. (Ascetic practices, like severe fasting, can induce hallucinations.)

From this interpretation one can see how the syncretistic philosophy had an impact on the Colossian Christians. It provided them regulations and means for participation with the angels in their heavenly worship. Thus the problem addressed in Colossians is not what some commentators suggest, namely the involvement of Christians in the worship of false-gods or sub-gods (*angels*). Rather the problem is Christological, for implicit in the Colossians' seeking to worship with the angels is the idea that to be united with Christ the Christian needs the mediation of some intermediate figure(s), here, angels.

Those Whom Colossians Opposes

Were there opponents, that is, outsiders, among the Colossians? It is difficult to answer this question from the information in Colossians. On the one hand, Colossians warns the readers,

"Look out lest there be someone robbing you . . ."

and

"Do not let anyone judge you . . ."

and

"Let no one give judgment against you. . . ."
But, on the other hand, there are no specific, strong statements lashing
out at opponents (in diatribe style) like those outbursts in 2 Corinthians, Galatians, and even 1 Thessalonians. What may be made of this?

It is possible, and from the tone in Colossians probable, that
outsider "philosophers" have come to the church, given their teaching,
and moved on. That the issue of *support* is not raised makes this
understanding more probable. But who are these people? One should
hold several facts in mind: (1) The asceticism is particularly Jewish
in character. (2) These "philosophers" were able to appeal to the Colossians who seem to have no other background in Judaism. (3) The
"philosophy" engaged in cosmic speculation. This combination of factors allows one to describe the "philosophers" as *Jewish Christian
syncretists*. They are not simply Jews, for the Colossian Christians
gave them a hearing and Colossians itself implies no movement from
Christianity to Judaism; nor are they Gnostics (nor even gnostic), for
there is no emphasis in Colossians on *gnosis*.

The Theology of the Opponents and the Problem

Certain elements of Jewish thought and practice have been given
a fresh interpretation in relation to Christ and have been fused with
popular cosmic speculation in order to produce a variety of Christianity
that is comfortable with its Jewish roots and its Hellenistic environment. We see here a hybrid: There is no scandal, no offense, no folly;
but rather there is a "vision" (2:18) and a method that guarantees some
result—perhaps a mystical experience or salvation, or both.

The Structure of the Letter

The structure of Colossians is difficult to discern. The letter
moves by thought association in the manner of an unfolding exposition
that is highly sermonic in character. In fact, scholars point to a variety
of traditional materials that have been incorporated into the letter.

Salutation. Colossians names Paul and Timothy as co-authors,
but the two are distinguished; for Timothy is Paul's "brother," whereas
Paul is "an apostle of Christ Jesus through the will of God" (1:1). The
writers and their designations are a verbatim match of 2 Cor 1:1a.

COLOSSIANS

Salutation	1:1–2
Thanksgiving	1:3–8
Body of the Letter	1:9–3:17
Parenesis	3:18–4:6
Closing	4:7–18

Colossians greets "those in Colossae who are saints and faithful brethren." The designations "saints" and "faithful brethren" are likely in reference to the same people, to whom the authors send "grace and peace from God our Father" (1:2).

Thanksgiving. In the next verses (1:3–8) the authors report their thankfulness, because of the Colossians' faith in the gospel of which they have heard. The reader learns that the Colossians "learned" the gospel from Epaphras.

The Body of the Letter. Scholars differ over what comprises the body of Colossians. Some designate 1:9–4:6 as the letter's body; others distinguish the doctrinally oriented material in 1:9–3:17 from the hortatory sections in 3:18–4:6, arguing that the latter is technically parenesis. Here we will focus only on the doctrinal material.

Col 1:9–14 expresses the authors' desire for the Colossians to be filled with the knowledge of God's will. Thus filled, the Colossians will have wisdom and understanding, and will live appropriately. Thereby the Colossians are told they may give thanks to God for their redemption, the forgiveness of their sins, which came to be by means of the delivery of Christians from darkness into the kingdom of God's Son.

In 1:12–20 the focus shifts to a grand Christological confession which includes a "hymn" in vv. 15–20. This early Christian liturgical piece declares the absolute finality of Christ and his superiority over all other "powers." Christ is confessed as being pre-existent, but his pre-existence is not passive existence alongside God, as in Phil 2:6–

11; rather he is active as the Head of creation. The hymn focuses on Christ in two moves, however, and says that as he was active in creation, so now he is active as the Head of a new corporate entity, namely the body of Christ which is *the Church*. Notice though that the Church is composed of "all things, whether on earth or in heaven," that are reconciled in and through Christ. Moreover, while the "hymn" proclaims Christ as (1) the Head of creation and (2) the Head of the Church, many unstated assumptions lie in the background. Something herein undeclared happened after Christ acted to create all things in heaven and on the earth: death entered the picture, a lack of peace came about, and there existed a need for reconciliation. In this situation, Christ the Head of creation acted as Christ the agent of cosmic redemption and is now Christ the Head of the Church. It is striking that the hymn does not attend to the problem; rather it dwells on the solution.

Col 1:21–23 takes the hymn as its point of departure and declares the reconciliation that Christ effected. But a hint of what is to follow comes here in the author's (the subject shifts here from "we" to "I, Paul") coupling a firm admonition to the readers to be steadfast with this grand pronouncement.

The next verses, from 1:24–2:5, do some traveling. First one reads of the work and suffering of the apostle for the disclosure of the mystery of God's word. This mystery is that Christ is in the Christian and thus the Christian has a hope for future glory. From this mentioning of the Christian's hope, the author expresses his overt desire to prevent the "delusion" of the Colossians (2:4).

After working up to the problem of the Colossians' being deluded, the letter engages in a give-and-take criticism of the demands of the "philosophy." The discussion refutes the "philosophy" in two parts. First, 2:6–15 explicates the significance of the full dominion of Jesus as Lord: in him is all divinity; thus he is over all and incorporates all; therefore "in him" Christians are freed from intermediaries and are in direct relation to the divine. Second, 2:16–23 says that for those who are in Christ (it is not clear who is *not* in him) there is no need or possibility of subjugation to lower universal powers. The argument is that Christians died with Christ to the rule of the powers and are raised with Christ (contrast Rom 6) into communion with him.

Col 3:1–17 is hortatory material, but it is doctrinal and abstract by comparison to the mundanely practical material that follows (3:18–4:6). In 3:1–4 the author declares that since Christians are raised with Christ they are to seek "heavenly" ways. This means, according to 3:5–17, that they are to put away (to death) the earthly (the impure) and are to have a new nature by putting on what they now know is *of* Christ. All this yields Christian praise.

Parenesis. Col 3:18–4:6 makes statements in fact about the new reality Christians have in Christ. First, 3:18–4:1 rehearses what appears to be a Christianized Stoic household code. The advice given assumes a distinction between that which is "earthly" and that which is "heavenly," or between the "old" and the "new." Moreover, God is conceived of as a God of orderliness and this section describes and advises a kind of order. Then, 4:2–6 remarks on the apostle's situation and issues a final admonition to *wise* conduct.

Closing. Colossians closes in five moves. (1) Tychichus and Onesimus, the bearers of the letter, are commended (4:7–9). (2) Extensive greetings from Paul's fellow workers are recorded, and the workers are distinguished as coming from those who are circumcised (Aristarchus, Mark, and Jesus Justus) or those who are not (Epaphras, Luke, and Demas) (4:10–15). (3) There is a general directive to exchange letters with the Laodiceans (4:16). (4) Specific directions are sent for Archippus (4:17). (5) Then "I, Paul" gives his autograph, calls for the remembrance of his bonds, and gives the benediction of grace.

The Solution or Advice Offered

Colossians is a kind of sermon, the theme of which is the grace of God, announced in 1:12–14. This announcement is followed by the quoting of a hymn (1:15–20), and this hymn becomes the text for the author's homiletical exposition. Notice that in the theme there is the idea that salvation is God's act of delivering the Christians from the dominion of darkness and transferring them to the kingdom of his Son. This is redemption, the forgiveness of sins. From this idea it becomes intelligible how and why baptism is treated as a rite of passage at 2:12 and 3:1.

Colossians takes this line in response to those who are delineating a plan (asceticism that brings one into the context of the worship of the angels) for ascending through the heavens. The letter does not deal with the problem in Colossae by resorting to exhortation alone; rather it takes the Colossians back to their baptism and preaches the gospel to them again!

Theological Keys to the Letter

Colossians makes several vital points:

1. Salvation is not the result of human effort but of the work of God.
2. The basis of God's work is the historical events of Christ, who was and is the one in whose flesh, by his death, the Christians (only?) were reconciled.
3. Thus the main emphasis of Colossians is Christological teaching.
   a. Christ is God's agent in creation.
   b. Christ is God's agent in reconciliation.
   c. So powerful is this reconciliation that it is cosmic in dimension, including even those forces that people of the Hellenistic era thought were alien and hostile.
   d. In Christ God restored harmony between himself and creation. Therefore, nothing intrudes in the heavens or on the earth between God, in Christ, and creation.
   e. No homage or concern is due to cosmic forces, angelic or demonic, for Christ is Head.
   f. Attached to the Head, the Church has no concern with or on account of extraterrestrial forces.
4. All this is what the Colossians already know; it is merely recalled in this letter.
5. The implications of this cosmic redemption are laid out in this letter in practical terms. The will of the author to be concrete about what redemption means produces internal tension in the letter itself, for the Stoic-like ordering of 3:18–4:1 and the distinctions made between the co-workers of "I, Paul" fall somewhat short of the vision expressed in 3:11, "Where [the new nature of Christ has been put on] one is not Greek and Jew, circumcised and uncircumcised, barbarian, Scythian, slave, free; rather Christ is all and in all."

BIBLIOGRAPHY

R. E. Brown, *The Churches the Apostles Left Behind* (New York: Paulist, 1984).

F. O. Francis, "Colossians, Letter to the," *IDBSup* 169–70.

Idem and W. A. Meeks, *Conflict at Colossae* (SBLSBS 4; Cambridge, Mass.: Society of Biblical Literature, 1973).

J. B. Lightfoot, *Saint Paul's Epistles to the Colossians and Philemon* (3d ed.; London: Macmillan, 1879).

E. Lohse, *Colossians and Philemon* (Hermeneia; Philadelphia: Fortress, 1971).

R. P. Martin, *Colossians: The Church's Lord and the Christian's Liberty* (Exeter: Paternoster, 1972).

E. Schweizer, *The Letter to the Colossians* (Minneapolis: Augsburg, 1982—German original 1976).

Ephesians

The so-called letter of Paul to the Ephesians is a multifaceted enigma. The oldest and best manuscripts do not include the words "in Ephesus (Greek: *en Ephesǭ*)" in Eph 1:1. This lack of specificity regarding the intended readers is symptomatic, for Ephesians is the least situational of all the New Testament letters attributed to Paul. Indeed the question is often raised whether Ephesians is a letter at all, for there is only the most general sort of salutation, no detectable problem exists among the readers, there is no closing greeting (Paul knew many people in Ephesus!), and the benediction is quite abstract. In fine, while Ephesians is a splendid writing, expressing some of the loftiest thoughts of early Christian triumphalism, it does not seem to be a letter. Rather R. H. Fuller seems correct when he calls Ephesians "a tract dressed up in epistolary form."

The Question of Authorship

We saw how and when Paul labored in Ephesus as we considered the background of his letters to Galatia and Corinth. It seems unwise to understand that this letter was originally directed to Ephesus, however, because of (1) the absence of "in Ephesus" in the best manuscripts, (2) the statement in 1:15 implying that the author knows the addressees only through hearsay, and (3) the corresponding statements in 3:2–13 that imply that the addressees know Paul only by hearsay. Thus it is unnecessary to rehash the Acts story, so this section takes up the difficult question of the authorship of Ephesians.

The majority of critical scholars (perhaps eighty to eighty-five percent) judge that Paul did not write Ephesians. Why?

The *vocabulary* of Ephesians does not cohere with Paul's general linguistic patterns. Forty-four words appear only in Ephesians among the letters attributed to Paul, and thirty-eight of these are *hapax legomena*. Even common Pauline words are replaced by otherwise non-Pauline synonyms and phrases—as examples notice, "devil (Greek: *diabolos*)" at 4:27 and 6:11 instead of the normal "Satan (Greek: *satanas*)"; "blood and flesh (Greek: *haima kai sarka*)" at 6:12 rather than simply "flesh"; and "heavenly places (Greek: *ta epouraniois*)" at 1:3, 20; 2:6; 3:10; and 6:12 rather than "heaven (Greek: *ouranos*)."

The *style* of Ephesians is remarkably different from the other letters. Here one finds a deliberate, florid prose involving non-Pauline syntax. There are long, nearly impossible sentences full of strings of nouns connected by prepositions and genitives—for example, both 1:3–10 and 2:1–7 are single rambling sentences in Greek. Throughout the epistle synonyms are heaped up in a labored way—see 3:6, even in English.

Another literary phenomenon that influences decisions concerning the Pauline authorship of Ephesians is the close literary relationship the letter has to Colossians. Though only Eph 6:21–22 agrees with Col 4:7 so exactly as to require literary dependence, seventy-three of the one hundred and fifty-five verses in Ephesians have verbal parallels to lines in Colossians. This contact is evident throughout Ephesians. Several major studies have addressed this issue, and the consensus is that Ephesians demonstrates a clear literary dependence on Colossians (see the bibliography), but it articulates significant developments of the theological thought expressed in Colossians itself. (In a similar, though less pronounced, way Ephesians shows verbal contacts with all the other Pauline letters except 2 Thessalonians.)

Above all the *theology* of Ephesians is developed so as to be different from Paul's normal thinking. Though the Christology of Ephesians has affinities with Colossians, it is heightened well beyond Colossians' expressions. In Colossians we saw Christ as the cosmic agent of redemption depicted as the Head of his body, the Church. But, in Ephesians, he is that and the Head of *all things,* for his body, the Church. Moreover he is the Groom of his bride, the Church, and the Cornerstone of the new, holy temple, the Church. This Christological heightening involves a parallel, heightened ecclesiology. In Ephesians "the Church" is purely an absolute term with no detectable reference to local communities of Christians. The Church is an over-arching, cosmic entity, referred to by a spate of images, like "the body of Christ," "the bride of Christ," "the household of God," "a holy temple," and "a dwelling place for God." Ephesians envisages the Church as that through which the multifarious wisdom of God is made known to the principalities and powers in the heavenly places (3:10). Simultaneously the status of the leaders of the Church is elevated. Apostles and prophets are described as the foundation of the Church as a holy temple (2:10). Indeed they are called "holy apostles and prophets" (3:5).

Other subtle (or not so subtle) theological shifts are noticeable. The hope of the *coming* of Christ is absent. There is no "coming one," and there is not only an "age to come," for 2:7 speaks of "the coming *ages*" wherein the future is secure for the Church. Moreover the Jew-Gentile issue is completely resolved (2:11–22), and Christians are *already* raised (2:5); indeed they are not merely experiencing the resurrection glory, but they are *already exalted with Christ,* seated with him in the heavenly places (2:6)!

All this illustrates the distinction between Ephesians and the other letters. If Paul wrote Ephesians he did so very late; in fact, the non-canonical early Christian materials concerning Paul that claim he was originally released by Nero and went to Spain before returning and dying in Rome must be correct, for it would require some time to move from the mind-set of the other letters to that expressed in Ephesians. If, on the other hand, Paul did not produce this letter, it is clear that it was produced by a dedicated student of his writings. For Ephesians shows a thorough knowledge of Paul's letters, while promulgating theological positions clearly developed beyond the thought in Paul's undisputed (and disputed) works. As before, no one factor settles the question of authorship, but the compendium of findings makes it most likely that Paul did not write this letter.

What Is Ephesians?

It is not entirely clear what the document called Ephesians was originally intended to do. Unlike the other Pauline letters, including even Romans, this piece does not seem to be related to any particular situation. Moreover there is no discernible theological controversy addressed, even abstractly. Thus if one is to state the purpose of Ephesians, it may be well to let the letter speak for itself. Ephesians synthesizes and develops themes in the earlier letters, presenting a kind of grand Pauline theology cast in the form of a standard Pauline communication. From observing what this "letter" *is*, perhaps one can say that the purpose of the author of Ephesians was to produce a document that did exactly what this one does, namely to synthesize, develop, and present Paul's thought in a new way for a new time and place.

The Structure of Ephesians

Ephesians falls into two broad parts. The first is theological exposition (1:1–3:21), and the second is extensive exhortations (4:1–6:20).

EPHESIANS	
Salutation	1:1–2
Thanksgiving	1:3–23
Body of the Letter	2:1–3:21
Parenesis	4:1–6:20
Closing	6:21–24

Salutation. The letter opens with an almost ideal "Pauline" greeting: Paul is identified as "an apostle of Christ Jesus through the will of God." Those addressed are "the saints, the faithful ones in Christ Jesus," and the greeting is that of "grace and peace" from God ("our Father") and ("the Lord Jesus") Christ.

Thanksgiving. This section comprises a psalm-like pronouncement (1:3–14; compare 2 Cor 1:3–11) that offers a doxology to God and a thanksgiving petition for the Christians' perception of the Christ-event (1:15–23). The petition is reminiscent of the thanksgiving in a number of other Pauline letters.

The Body of the Letter. This section runs from 2:1 through 3:21

and falls into four broad parts. First, 2:1–10 declares that the work of Christ amounts to the movement from death to life for those who are saved. Next, 2:11–22 ruminates upon the absolute reconciliation of the circumcised and the uncircumcised, calling the two "one new man" and referring to the reconciliation as the making of "peace." Then 3:1–13 takes up Paul's ministry and his fate of suffering. Notice here the emphasis on "I, Paul" having "insight into the mystery of Christ" (3:4), an insight that should be evident from reading what is written in Ephesians (3:3)! In other words, Ephesians claims to lay out the mystery. Finally 3:14–21 offers another lofty, though personal, thanksgiving prayer.

Parenesis. Like Colossians, to which it has many affinities, Ephesians includes detailed moral observations and instructions. The exhortations begin with a summons to "unity in the Spirit in the bond of peace" (4:1–10). Eph 4:11–16 takes up the gifts of God for the upbuilding of the Church, a growth into unity in Christ. Warnings are issued in 4:17–24 against immoral living. Proscriptions against certain activities are coupled with prescriptions of other, commendable endeavors in 4:25–5:20 before the letter offers a Christian (Christianized Stoic) household code in 5:21–6:9. An admonition to be prepared for engagement in the cosmic battle between God and the "evil one" makes up 6:10–17. Finally Ephesians directs the reader to "pray at all times in the Spirit" for themselves and the apostle as those engaged in the battle (6:18–20).

Closing. The letter concludes with a recommendation of Tychichus (6:21–22) and a benediction of "peace" and "grace" (6:23–24)— a reversal of the order, grace and peace, in the salutation. This brings Ephesians full circle to its close.

The Theology and Morality of Ephesians

The author of Ephesians is smitten by a single theme, *reconciliation*. This idea is worked out in terms of cosmic unity in and through Christ. This central theme is a *leitmotiv* which may be viewed from several angles.

(1) Much is made of the person of Christ, especially on a cosmic scale: He is the one in whom God has united all things, in heaven and on earth (1:10); thus he is the Head of all things (1:22).

(2) Christ is the Head over all things "for the Church" (1:22) which is his body, and Christ's body is cosmic in scale (1:23). Indeed Christ and the cosmic Church are practically one entity. But notice the make-up of the Church. It is composed both of reconciled Jew and Gentile (2:16) and of the heavenly and the earthly (1:10).

(3) The vision is clearly that of the achievement of cosmic hegemony. We see a cosmic Christ working a work of cosmic reconciliation that is the uniting of all things, not only *in* heaven and *on* earth, but *of heaven and earth themselves.*

A Key to Ephesians

One must recognize that Ephesians is lofty stuff! It is close, on the one hand, to gnosticism with its emphasis on the mystery of Christ which the apostle has and which he communicates in this letter to the readers. In a sense Ephesians is clearly thought to be a privileged communication. Yet part and parcel of this marvelous message is a feature that radically distinguishes Ephesians from true Gnosticism, namely, extensive moral exhortations. In Ephesians, the mystery is articulated, and it comes with a catalogue of social and spiritual duties for the Christians living in a new age of reconciliation. Here is a line of teaching far from the typical gnostic emphasis on privilege alone!

BIBLIOGRAPHY

T. K. Abbott, *Epistles to the Ephesians and Colossians* (ICC; Edinburgh: Clark, 1897).

M. Barth, *Ephesians,* 2 Vols. (AB 34 and 34A; Garden City: Doubleday, 1974).

N. A. Dahl, "Ephesians, Letter to the," *IDBSup* 268–69.

J. P. Sampley, "The Letter to the Ephesians" in J. P. Sampley, *et al., Ephesians, Colossians, 2 Thessalonians, The Pastoral Epistles* (Proclamation Commentaries; Philadelphia: Fortress, 1978) 9–39.

R. H. Fuller, *A Critical Introduction to the New Testament* (London: Duckworth, 1966).

The Pastoral Epistles

In 1753 a German scholar, Paul Anton, designated 1 Timothy, 2 Timothy, and Titus "the pastorals," and subsequent scholarship has perpetuated this name. Anton referred to these three letters in this fashion because he observed that the letters came from a pastor, Paul, to other pastors, Timothy and Titus, concerning the pastoral activity of building up the church. The writings clearly belong together, for they cohere in terms of vocabulary, style, and theological perspective in such a manner that they form a distinct cluster within the letters of the New Testament attributed to Paul.

Indeed issues of language, style, and theology in the pastorals provide the fodder for scholarly skepticism concerning Pauline authorship. Moreover each of the letters presents itself as coming from a time in the life of Paul that is not addressed by the other Pauline letters or Acts. Paul appears to have been acquitted when he went to Rome, to have made a subsequent missionary journey to the eastern part of the Mediterranean, and then to have been jailed a second time in Rome. The linguistic, stylistic (grammar and syntax), and theological arguments concerning Pauline authorship of the pastorals have been the subject of many significant scholarly studies and are fully rehearsed in all standard New Testament introductions—for example, see W. G. Kümmel, *Introduction* 366–87—and so there is no need to repeat the arguments here. Suffice it to say that over ninety percent of critical scholars judge that the pastorals do not come from Paul.

Nevertheless, among the ten percent who do affirm Pauline authorship are prominent scholars like D. Guthrie, J. Jeremias, and J. N. D. Kelly. These critics argue persuasively that the pastorals do not fit the historical situation of the later patristic writings, even as early as Clement of Rome (c. A.D. 96) or Ignatius of Antioch (c. A.D. 107). Thus it seems that H. Koester and others who argue for a date for the composition of the pastorals between A.D. 120–160 do not have a strong case. Yet this is all that the argument in relation to patristic writings can demonstrate, for demonstrating that the pastorals are not necessarily from the patristic era does not prove their Pauline origin. Considering all the evidence, it seems R. H. Fuller is correct when he observes that the pastorals articulate a church order developed beyond Paul but more primitive than that of Ignatius; and, therefore, these letters were most likely written during the generation after Paul and before Ignatius, between A.D. 65–90. I favor a time toward the middle-to-end of this period because the church order of the pastorals would have taken some time to develop after the death of Paul, and it seems even more developed than the order presupposed in Acts which itself probably comes from A.D. 80–90.

Those to Whom the Letters Are
Addressed and the Situations Envisaged

To begin study of the pastorals, one should ask what can be known about those to whom the letters are addressed and what setting in life is presupposed by the pastorals themselves.

Timothy. From the undisputed letters of Paul one learns that Timothy was one of Paul's fellow workers (1 Thess 1:1; 1 Cor 4:17; 2 Cor 1:1; Rom 16:21; Phil 1:1; Phlm 1). He served as Paul's agent on some occasions (1 Thess 3:2; 1 Cor 4:17; Phil 2:19) and is named as co-author of several of the letters (1 Thess 1:1; 2 Cor 1:1; Phil 1:1; Phlm 1). In addition Timothy's name is given as a co-author of Colossians.

From Acts, especially chapter 16, one learns complementary information about Timothy. He was from Derbe-Lystra, his mother was Jewish and his father Greek, and before he became a partner with Paul on the mission field Paul circumcised him (many scholars question this information).

Timothy's Situation According to 1 and 2 Timothy. 1 Timothy depicts Paul as having left Timothy in Ephesus (1:3–4) when he went to Macedonia. Now the apostle writes (3:14) in order that Timothy "may know how one ought to conduct oneself in the household of God, which is the church . . ." (3:15).

In 2 Timothy one finds a different situation. Here Paul is in prison in Rome (1:16–17; 2:9), but Timothy may still be portrayed as being in Ephesus (1:18; 4:19?). Paul has had one hearing that went well despite adverse circumstances (4:16–18), but at the time of the writing the apostle foresees his death (4:6–8). He writes to Timothy with personal advice and a series of warnings about problems in the church. Finally he beckons Timothy to come to him (4:9) and asks that Timothy bring him certain items (4:13).

Titus. In the undisputed letters one finds that Titus was one of Paul's fellow workers (2 Cor 8:6) and that he served as Paul's emissary, especially for the collection (2 Cor 8:6, 16, 23) and in the controversial exchange between Paul and the Corinthians (2 Cor 12:18; 2:13; 7:6, 13–14). In addition one learns that Titus was a Greek, that he was uncircumcised, that he accompanied Paul when the apostle went to Jerusalem for the apostolic council there, and that he was not compelled to be circumcised (Gal 2:1–3).

Titus' Situation According to Titus. Paul is portrayed as being in Nicopolis (3:12), a city in northwest Greece in the Roman province of Epirus, a region bordering on the Ionian Sea. The apostle has left Titus on Crete (1:5) to direct the development of the church there. The letter gives advice on church order, for church members, for Titus himself, and issues warnings about problems in the church. The letter informs Titus that later the apostle will send for him to come to Nicopolis (3:12).

The Problems or Situations Eliciting the Letters

The pastorals depict Paul thinking of the companions he has left behind in ministry situations (1 Timothy and Titus) or of the church(es) that will remain after his death (2 Timothy). From both perspectives the apostle is shown to express his concern about the danger of the Christians being misled by false teachers into a perversion of true Christianity—see especially 1 Tim 4:1–2; 2 Tim 3:6; 4:3; Titus 1:1.

But notice the different emphases in these letters. 2 Timothy deals primarily with heresy or false teaching and doctrine, whereas 1 Tim-

othy and Titus are concerned primarily with church order in organization and doctrine, and only secondarily do they take up heresy
(though the possibility of heresy may be a major motivation for the
production of these letters delineating church order).

The Opponents and Their Theology

We actually learn the names of some of those whom "Paul" opposes in these letters. 1 Tim 1:20 names Hymenaeus and Alexander
as two who have rejected "conscience" and who need "to learn not to
blaspheme." 2 Tim 2:17–18 tells of Hymenaeus (obviously a pesti-
ferous fellow!) and Philetus who have said the resurrection has already
passed. This reminds us of the problem in 2 Thessalonians (and perhaps 1 Corinthians). Then, 2 Tim 4:14 refers to one Alexander who
did the apostle great harm and promises that the Lord will give him
his due. This promise of divine retribution is also reminiscent of
2 Thessalonians (see 2 Thess 1:6).

Nevertheless, the identity of the "heresies" opposed throughout
the letters is quite difficult to determine in theological terms. On the
one hand, the descriptions of the problems seem typical of things related to Jews or Jewish-Christian groups. Phrases that suggest such a
background include:

"teachers of the law" (1 Tim 1:7);

"abstinence from food" (1 Tim 4:3);

"the circumcision party" (Titus 1:10);

"Jewish myths" (Titus 1:14); and

"quarrels over the law" (Titus 3:9).

On the other hand, the references to the problems seem characteristic
of or suggest an association with gnostic-like thought:

"myths" (1 Tim 1:4; 4:7; 2 Tim 4:4);

"genealogies and speculation" (1 Tim 1:4);

"forbid marriage" (1 Tim 4:3);

"godless chatter"
  = "knowledge" (1 Tim 6:20–21);
  = "the resurrection has already passed" (2 Tim 2:16–17);
"commands of people rejecting the truth" (Titus 1:14).

Both elements are brought together under the mud-slinging of 2 Tim 2:23; 3:1–9; and they are covered by blanket terms in other places. "Vain discussions" at 1 Tim 1:7 takes in myths, genealogies, speculation, and teachers of the law. "Deceitful spirits and the doctrine of demons" at 1 Tim 4:1–2 covers both abstinence from food and forbidding marriage. "Stupid controversies, genealogies, dissensions, and quarrels over the law" form one big lump at Titus 3:9.

All this may point to quasi-gnostic Jewish Christians (a phenomenon somewhat similar to that behind Colossians) against whom the pastorals rail and of whom they warn. Yet the pastorals may not describe any one particular group but rather refer generally to phenomena of heresy and cite a few, various examples. It seems impossible to decide based upon present information. In any case the pastorals do not give a specific description of "a heresy" and do not offer a specific refutation of a particular problem. Indeed it should be noticed that while the author of the pastorals is distressed by heretical teaching per se, the moral failure of the "heretics" is at least as great a cause for concern as the content of the erroneous teaching. Right thought and living are inseparably bonded in the mind of the author as are perverse thought and life.

Solution or Advice

One observes a shift in the image of Paul in the pastorals from *apostle-missionary* to *pastor*, from *crusader* to *administrator*. Moreover the answer to the problem(s) is not Paul's usual one of debate with the other position by expounding upon the Christ-event and the peculiarities of the power of God. Here there is no argument but, rather, denunciation and advice toward defensive measures. The vision is this: Some Pauline communities are deficient and particularly vulnerable in that they do not have proper local authorities. Now (as seen in Titus 1:5, 7) the need is met, the solution is supplied, as "presbyter-bishops" are appointed in every church.

The solution is one of structured morality. Although 1 Tim 3:2 and Titus 1:9 reveal that bishops "teach" and 1 Tim 3:5; 5:17 show that presbyter-bishops "rule," one learns far less about the duties these officers have than about the character they must possess. In summary, the appointed leader is to live up to the following description:

blameless,
upright,
holy,
self-controlled,
not arrogant,
without a quick temper,
able to manage his own household,
in control of his children,
cannot be a lover of money,
cannot be a drunk,
cannot have been married more than once,
cannot be a recent convert,
his children must be Christians,
well thought of by outsiders,
sensible,
dignified,
hospitable,
an apt teacher.

(Notice that Paul would flunk this test! For he was not without a temper; he began to preach as a recent "convert," and at times his letters are less than fully dignified.)

The reader of the pastorals also learns of "deacons" and "widows"—also early Christian offices. But it is not entirely clear from the letters what these people did.

A Key to the Pastorals

In a nutshell the pastorals make an effort to insure qualified leadership for the church. A key word is *stability*. The vision is of a Christian community whose harmonious life will be facilitated by sound leadership.

While a reading of the pastorals shows an emphasis upon leaders with personal stability who can by virtue of their personal integrity guarantee sound doctrine, this is not the sole interest of these letters. For the sound teaching or "true faith" is itself a major concern of the author. Strikingly the letters do not attempt to communicate the content of this doctrine. Instead they assume that the recipients/readers know what true faith is. What is clear herein is that Christian faith is not merely to be propagated but is to be preserved against corruption from within and attack from without (see 1 Tim 1:3–4, 19; 3:9, 15; 4:1, 6–7; 6:10, 12, 14, 20; 2 Tim 1:13–14; 2:15, 18; 3:14–17; 4:3–4; Titus 1:9, 13; 2:1–2)—a sentiment that, in principle, Paul would applaud. Thus, ultimately the church leaders serve the "pure faith" in seeing that it is fixed, held, and defended.

BIBLIOGRAPHY

M. Dibelius and H. Conzelmann, *The Pastoral Epistles* (Hermeneia; Philadelphia: Fortress, 1972).

R. H. Fuller, "The Pastoral Epistles" in J. P. Sampley, *et al.*, *Ephesians, Colossians, 2 Thessalonians, The Pastoral Epistles* (Proclamation Commentaries; Philadelphia: Fortress, 1978) 97–121.

Pauline Theology: An Overview of Paul's Thought

The following portion of this book is a treatment of Pauline theology. For the work done in this section, earlier decisions about the authorship of the canonical Pauline epistles play an important role, since the theological reflections presented here are developed only from the seven undisputed letters. From time to time the other letters are mentioned in order to contrast their theological positions with those of the undisputed letters, but they are not taken as primary material for explicating Paul's thinking on the topics considered below.

This "Pauline theology" is perhaps unorthodox in more ways than one, but in general it differs from other such statements in that it approaches theological topics seeking merely to articulate what Paul thought and wrote on particular, important, diverse subjects. As throughout the rest of this book, the apocalyptic framework of Paul's thought forms the foundation of the study. This foundation provides some unity for the section, but it will not alleviate all frustration. Problems are raised, but they are not always solved; for frequently Paul did not say enough about vital theological issues for one ever to know exactly what he thought.

Moreover this section does not seek to exhaust every issue of Pauline theology or to synthesize Paul's thinking into a true system.

Paul's thought is pondered and explicated, as possible, but neither at the expense of allowing real enigmas in the apostle's thought to remain enigmatic nor by making truly ambiguous matters less than ambiguous. Readers be forewarned: you will probably like or hate this part of the book.

The Righteousness of God

Much of the recent literature on Pauline theology relates to Paul's phrase "the righteousness of God." Scholars debate the meaning of these words, for in Greek (*dikaiosynē theou,* hereafter *dTh*) they are sufficiently ambiguous to allow for various interpretations. Two of these, the interpretation of the genitive phrase *dTh* as either a "subjective" or "objective" genitive, determine the major poles of this debate. This grammatical terminology often obscures rather than clarifies the distinctions interpreters strive to make. Thus in what follows the term *subjective genitive* is used but the phrase *genitive of authorship* appears in the place of the somewhat misleading term *objective genitive.* To explain further: by *subjective genitive* interpreters indicate that *dTh* means "the righteousness which belongs to God and proceeds from him," and by *genitive of authorship* they understand the sense of *dTh* as "the righteousness which is acceptable in God's eyes and bestowed by him upon us." Another way to clarify the difference between these two interpretations is to illustrate each alternative by constructing explanatory sentences. *DTh* as a subjective genitive means "God is righteous," and the interpretation of the phrase as a genitive of authorship indicates that "God gives righteousness." Although these distinctions rest upon seemingly subtle grammatical points they do more than argue for particular linguistic nuances. The implications of the interpretation of *dTh* as either a subjective genitive or a genitive of authorship are enormous, *for in Paul's writings "the righteousness of God" is integrally related to salvation.*

Interpreters who argue that the genitive phrase *dTh* is a genitive of authorship generally see salvation in relation to *human possibility.* In this frame of reference "righteousness" is a gift from God that

comes to the person of faith. The faith of the individual is the attitude
of the person in which the gift of salvation is accomplished. Simply
stated, faith becomes the condition for the reception of righteousness
by the individual. On the other hand, those exegetes who contend that
"the righteousness of God" is a subjective genitive think of salvation
in relation to *God's power*. In the context of this interpretation "righteousness" is a way of referring to God's saving activity. This saving
activity is the means by which God subordinates creation to his lordship and by which humanity becomes responsible to God. Faith in this
instance is created by the saving activity of God, i.e., faith is the
product of "the righteousness of God."

In order to understand "the righteousness of God" in the writings
of Paul, it is necessary to be aware of some of the scholarly debate
concerning *dTh*. Therefore, a survey of the contours of a portion of
the debate follows. Then we shall briefly examine Paul's uses of the
phrase "the righteousness of God," and, finally, we shall consider the
synthetic task of Pauline theology with respect to the idea of "the
righteousness of God."

The Debate

The interest in the meaning of the phrase "the righteousness of
God" extends back to the earliest period of recorded biblical interpretation. During the period from the apostolic fathers until the Reformation there were two established, recurring, and interlacing attempts
at interpretation of *dTh*. The first and predominant explanation of "the
righteousness of God" was as a sort of abbreviation for the concept
of the *justice of God*. In other words, "the righteousness of God" was
thought to be God's distributive judicial fairness or God's *impartiality
in judgment*. According to the apostolic fathers it is this distributive
justice that brings about the happening of justification. In this regard
"the righteousness of God" as an abbreviation for God's judicial equity
was thought *to denote God's gift*. With Augustine, however, one fully
encounters this second element of interpretation. In his reflection upon
"the righteousness of God" Augustine explained *dTh* to be *God's gift
of righteousness that justifies belief*. In other words, "the righteousness
of God" signifies or designates God's mercy itself. Augustine alone,

prior to the Reformation, saw that God's mercy and God's righteousness hang together.

It was Martin Luther who first and consistently rendered *dTh* as an objective genitive, or, by the definition of terms given above, a genitive of authorship. He argued that "the righteousness of God" is that righteousness that counts before God and that humanity possesses as a gift from God. With his major emphasis on the gift quality of "the righteousness of God," Luther associated righteousness and creation in an effort toward mutual interpretation. This interpretative joining of righteousness and creation allowed for the interpretation of *iustitia Dei* as God's work of gracious, creative redemption that God performs in behalf of humanity.

During this century the legacy of Luther was received, developed, and expounded in its most significant form by Rudolf Bultmann. From his characteristic, anthropological starting point, in the terminology and upon the framework of existential philosophy, Bultmann argues that "the righteousness of God" is a "forensic eschatological term" that Paul had in common with his Jewish heritage. According to Bultmann, what distinguishes Paul's use of the term *dTh* from standard Jewish employment is that "what for most Jews is a *matter of hope* is for Paul *a present reality*— or, better, is also a present reality." Within Bultmann's system of interpretation, righteousness is primarily related to the *human possibility* of salvation (or, authentic existence). The individual is *righteous* not to the extent that he/she may *be* righteous, but to the extent that he/she is *acknowledged* innocent by God. "Therefore, the righteousness which God adjudicates to man (the man of faith) is not 'sinlessness' in the sense of ethical perfection, but is 'sinlessness' in the sense that God does not 'count' man's sins against him (II Cor 5:19)." The fundamental distinction Bultmann sees between Paul and Judaism concerning righteousness is not, however, the difference between *present reality* and *future hope,* but is the condition to which God's acquitting decision is tied. The *future hope* of Judaism is directly related to the law while the possible *present reality* which Paul proclaimed comes *sola fide* from grace. Bultmann holds that righteousness has its origin in God's grace and, therefore, is *called* God's righteousness. The phrase "the righteousness of God" is, then, a genitive of authorship and "God's righteousness" means the righteousness from God which is conferred upon humanity as a gift by God's free grace alone.

The most forceful refutation of Bultmann's program of interpretation of "the righteousness of God" is the work of Ernst Käsemann, who understands *dTh* to be a key phrase for comprehending the writings of Paul. Thus he labors at length to interpret this phrase with fidelity to Paul's intention. Käsemann contends that "the righteousness of God" was not a term invented by Paul; rather Paul found this phrase as a ready-made term in apocalyptic Judaism. Käsemann traces the background of the phrase from its literary origin at Deut 33:21, through the *Testament of Dan* 6:10, to 1QS 11:12. He contends that "the formulation which Paul has taken over speaks primarily of God's saving activity, which is present in his gift as a precipitate without being completely dissolved into it." In other words, Käsemann emphasized that the gift-dimension of God's righteousness is inseparable from the Giver. Thus, "the righteousness of God" is not a divine property, characteristic of a Greek god; and so, it cannot be made-over to a human *as if* that human possessed the property. Rather, "the righteousness of God" speaks of God's divine activity: "God's sovereignty over the world revealing itself eschatologically in Jesus." For Käsemann, "the righteousness of God" is God's *victorious, creation-covenant-faithful power-action:* it is a salvation-creating activity. Moreover, this salvation-creating activity is an apocalyptic event that brings about the shift of the aeons. "The righteousness of God" is cosmic in scope, and it provides the believer with the certitude of faith but not with absolute certainty. Käsemann sees Paul speaking from an apocalyptic perspective and announcing "the righteousness of God" which demonstrates that "God's power reaches out for the world, and the world's salvation lies in its being recaptured for the sovereignty of God. For this very reason it is the gift of God and also the salvation of the individual human being when we become obedient to the divine righteousness."

Käsemann's interpretation of "the righteousness of God" as the salvation-creating power-action of God has drawn both criticism and support. A notable critique was offered by Bultmann who states that Käsemann's conclusions do not follow his evidence. Bultmann argues that while the gift of righteousness is the result of God's action toward the human individual, the term *righteousness* does not necessarily describe the action per se. He claims that while "the righteousness of God" does appear as a generic term in Jewish literature, it does not occur in relation to a present reality as it does in Paul's writings. Therefore, *dī'h* is not a radicalizing and universalizing of a Jewish term; rather it is a fresh creation of Paul.

Nevertheless, Käsemann is unswerving in his commitment to the interpretation of "the righteousness of God" as creative, cosmic, redemptive activity that allows for no separation between gift and Giver. He defends his position against the censure of both Bultmann and other critics. One quotation demonstrates his assurance that his interpretation is correct and helps to clarify his position:

> That God's grace and righteousness relate to the world and intend a new creation, not merely a number of believing individuals, seems to me an irrelinquishable truth if the Christian proclamation is to be the foundation of anything more than merely private piety. I must once more replace the alternatives by a dialectic. The justification of the ungodly certainly in the first place affects, in concrete terms, myself. But the phrase is robbed of its full significance if it does not mean salvation for everyone and for the whole world. For even the ungodly only exist, in a remarkable transsubjective way, in the entanglement of all earthly things in sin and death.

Support for Käsemann's explanation of "the righteousness of God" in Paul's thought comes in the works of both Roman Catholic and Protestant scholars who appropriate various aspects of this interpretation in order to articulate their own interpretations. These subsequent constructions differ from Käsemann's not so much in kind as in their particular emphases. But, despite the enormous support which Käsemann's thesis has gained, certain exegetes continue to deny the correctness of his interpretation and to depreciate his interpretative program. They seek chiefly to shatter the unity of justification and sanctification that Käsemann claims to have established. This supposed disintegration intends to make anew the provision for *human autonomy*.

"The Righteousness of God" in Paul's Letters

To work through this debated topic it seems advisable to analyze Paul's own use of the phrase, *dTh*. I do not attempt full-scale exegetical treatments of the relevant texts here, but six passages demand some comment.

2 Cor 5:11–21. In 2 Cor 5:11–21 one sees that "the righteousness of God" is spoken of as the manifestation of the Christian community (the whole Church). The existence of the community is related to God's saving activity, and thus "the righteousness of God" in this passage denotes God's saving power.

Romans. At four distinct points in his letter to the church at Rome, Paul speaks of "the righteousness of God." Rom 1:16–17; 3:1–8; and 3:21–26 speak of "the righteousness of God" as being revealed, being shown, and being made manifest. "The righteousness of God" in each of these instances is obviously a definite conceptual entity within Paul's thought world. Rom 1:16–17 emphasized the faithfulness of God in terms of "the righteousness of God" and in such a manner that it connotes God's saving power. Rom 3:1–8 relates the truth and faithfulness of God to "the righteousness of God." The truth, faithfulness, and righteousness are such that they (it?) overcome the lie, unfaithfulness, and unrighteousness of humanity. Again, the saving power of God is connoted by Paul's language. Rom 3:21–26 speaks of "the righteousness of God" in such a way that what is being manifested is the self-expression of God. This self-expression is God's action in saving humanity, so again the saving-power character of God is connoted by "the righteousness of God." Finally, Rom 10:1–4 offers an occurrence of the phrase *dTh* that leaves no doubt that "the righteousness of God" is God's power at work unto salvation.

Phil 3:2–11. In these verses the term "the righteousness of God" does not occur exactly; rather, the phrase *tēn ek theou dikaiosynēn* ("the righteousness from/out of God") appears. Therefore, whatever may be said about these verses must be considered in light of the inexactness of this passage for a strict consideration of "the righteousness of God." Nevertheless, in this passage Paul sums up his experience of "righteousness *from* God" using a present passive participle, "*being* conformed to his death" (v. 10). Thus, Paul clearly does not portray himself as the rightwising force; rather, God is the power related to righteousness.

The Results. This brief survey points to a clear conclusion: *"the righteousness of God" in the writings of Paul means the saving power of God that is at work in the world unto salvation.* When one ponders this finding in relation to the ideas of salvation as either a human possibility *or* the result of divine power, one sees that an interpretation of "the righteousness of God" in terms of human possibility ignores the texts that speak most explicitly about "the righteousness of God." The interpretative work of Bultmann and others seems to go astray at the outset when it starts with the general category of "righteousness" and considers "the righteousness of God" as a subheading under that larger, general topic, a move that deprives *dTh* of its peculiar force.

Seeing that "the righteousness of God" is related to God's saving power and not to human possibility allows one to decide whether faith is a condition for (as the appropriate human attitude for reception of salvation) or a result of, or, better, a characteristic of, salvation. The text of Rom 3:21–26 makes it clear that faith is created by God's saving activity (this observation is confirmed by Paul's inclusion of *pistis* ["faith"] as a fruit of the Spirit in Gal 5:22). It is God's faithfulness ("the righteousness of God" as saving activity) that overcomes human faithlessness. Thus, from a study of the texts dealing with *dTh*, especially Rom 3:21–26, one learns that faith is not a condition *for* reception of salvation but is the condition *of* (or that characterizes) salvation. Moreover, one sees that it is the interpretation of Käsemann rather than Bultmann that is accurate exegetically with regard to the role of faith.

It is not merely by chance that those who understand "the righteousness of God" to be a genitive of authorship and who think of salvation in relation to human possibility tend to devaluate the apocalyptic aspect of the thought of the apostle Paul, while those who explain "the righteousness of God" as a subjective genitive and who view salvation in relation to God's power articulate the essential importance of apocalyptic for a correct interpretation of Paul's writings.

Conclusions

The findings and insights gained to this point lead one to the broad question, "What forms the center of Paul's theology?" One sees that "the righteousness of God" is *a* central motif in the thought of Paul. The question, however, is whether or not *dTh* is *the* central category in Paul's thought. By careful examination of the phrase *dTh* in Paul's letters, one sees that for Paul "the righteousness of God" is *a code-term for the consistent vision of the salvific triumph of God.* If, as J. C. Beker seems correctly to have demonstrated, *this vision forms the coherent center* of all that the apostle has to say, then one may conclude that the phrase *"the righteousness of God" is the key category in Paul's thought.*

BIBLIOGRAPHY

J. C. Beker, *Paul the Apostle* (2d ed.; Philadelphia: Fortress, 1984).

R. Bultmann, *Theology of the New Testament,* I (New York: Scribner's Sons, 1951).

Idem, "DIKAINOSYNĒ THEOU," *JBL* 83 (1964) 12–16.

E. Käsemann, *New Testament Questions of Today* (Philadelphia: Fortress, 1969).

Idem, Perspectives on Paul (Philadelphia: Fortress, 1969).

G. Klein, "Righteousness in the New Testament," *IDBSup* 750–52.

M. L. Soards, "The Righteousness of God in the Writings of the Apostle Paul," *BTB* 15 (1985) 104–109.

The Gospel and Christology

We have seen that apocalyptic eschatology forms the framework of Paul's thinking about God and that the substance of the apostle's understanding of God is summed up in the phrase "the righteousness of God." But there is nothing uniquely Christian about these concepts; in fact, one might argue that Paul shares these ideas with Judaism. Yet Paul understands his "good news" to be absolutely Christian, and he fights for his basic belief that there is only one gospel, namely, what God did and does in Jesus Christ. This good news is not theology per se, yet it implies a particular understanding of God, Christ, and the human situation. Thus we must consider the particularly Christian element(s) of Paul's thought by focusing on Paul's *Christology*.

Paul on Jesus Christ

"Christ" means "messiah" and is a title designating "the anointed one (of God)." The man to whom Paul ascribes this title is Jesus. In other words, Paul believes and proclaims that Jesus is the anointed one of God.

From this observation comes another which is sometimes unsettling: it is remarkable that Paul demonstrates so little knowledge about Jesus! He knows Jesus was a Jew, for he writes that Jesus was a descendant of Abraham (Gal 3:16), from the line of David (Rom 1:3), an Israelite (Rom 9:5). Paul knows Jesus had a family, since he says he was born of a woman (Gal 4:4) and had brothers (1 Cor 9:5), one of whom was James of Jerusalem (Gal 1:19; 2:6, 9). Furthermore Paul says that Jesus had a ministry to his own people, the Jews (Rom 15:8), and that Jesus' life ended as he was crucified by the rulers of this age

(1 Cor 2:8). Finally Paul says Jesus was dead and buried (1 Cor 8:11; 1 Cor 15:4). This is what Paul shows that he knows about Jesus.

A common response to this observation is the claim that Paul certainly knew more about Jesus than he relates in his letters, that is, Paul did not write everything he knew. The problem here—I do not wish to appear overly skeptical, but—the problem is that one cannot know that Paul knew more than he wrote, because what he wrote is all one has. Nevertheless, many scholars find allusions to the historical Jesus in Paul's letters and insist that the letters reveal Paul knew more than is obvious. But L. E. Keck is correct when he says, "The more one studies such attempts to locate allusions, the more skeptical one becomes."

What positive use can we make of this seeming dearth of information about Jesus in Paul's letters? It seems that for Paul the historical Jesus is framed by the pre-existence of God's Son and the post-existence of the resurrected, exalted Lord. Thus a synthetic sketch of what Paul did know about the whole story of Jesus Christ has the following lines:

1. Christ pre-existed (Phil 2:6);
2. God sent the Son forth (Gal 4:4; Rom 8:3–4);
3. he was born by a human mother (Gal 4:4);
4. he lived as a Jew (Gal 4:4; Rom 1:3) and had a family (1 Cor 9:5; Gal 1:19);
5. he instituted the Lord's Supper (1 Cor 11:23–26);
6. he was betrayed (1 Cor 11:23);
7. he was crucified (Gal 3:13; 1 Cor 2:2);
8. he died (1 Cor 8:11; Rom 5:6);
9. he was buried (1 Cor 15:4; Rom 6:4);
10. he was raised from the dead by God (1 Thess 1:10);
11. he was/is exalted by God (Phil 2:9);
12. he is present in heaven at the right hand of God—there he reigns (1 Cor 15:23), destroying every rule, authority, and power (1 Cor 15:24) and interceding for God's elect (Rom 8:34);
13. he will descend/come from heaven on the day of the Lord (1 Thess 4:16; 1 Cor 15:23);
14. he will achieve universal hegemony (1 Cor 15:24; Phil 2:10–11); and then

15. he will hand over the kingdom to God (1 Cor 15:24); and finally
16. he will himself be subjected to God (1 Cor 15:28).

For Paul what matters is the whole of this scheme. One part is not more important than the others (though we will see that a key exists that unlocks the meaning of the whole), for Paul is concerned with what God did and does in and through Jesus Christ, not merely what the human Jesus did.

Keys to Paul's Christology

Two of the weightiest aspects of Paul's thought and teaching about Christ are the *sending* of God's Son and his subsequent *death*.

Paul on the Sending of God's Son. At Gal 4:4 and Rom 8:3–4 the apostle speaks about God sending his Son. Scholars see reflected in these statements pre-Pauline tradition(s), for the syntax of the statements appears to follow a set formula wherein

——God is the subject;
——the verb is "to send" (*exapostellein* in Gal 4; *pempein* in Rom 8);
——the object of the sending is the Son;
——a purpose (*hina*) clause or clauses follow, explaining the soteriological significance of the sending.

Striking parallels to the thought expressed in this particular formulation are found in the literature of Hellenistic Judaism as represented by Philo (*Somn.* 1.69), Sirach (24), Baruch (3), and Wisdom (9). In these sources God sends *Torah* or *Wisdom* or *the Logos* for the salvation of humankind. This probably indicates that the idea of salvific sending was available to early Christianity from its cultural milieu, but the Christian expression of this notion is distinctive in two ways. First, the idea is related to a specific historical human figure, Jesus, and, second, the triumph which eventuates from the sending and which is applied to humanity is over or in relation to the law! Thus the proclamation of Paul shows a radical reappropriation of the sending formula. The apostle not only "demythologizes" the formula by saying that the sent-one is identical with Jesus, he says the sending brought liberation from the very thing that is elsewhere said to have been sent for humanity's salvation, namely, the law.

Thus the sending is not merely prophetic proclamation ("Thus saith the Lord!"), or divine illumination (providing Torah, Wisdom, or Logos). The sending of God's Son is a concrete act that *achieves* salvation for humanity; it is the good news, "Thus doth the Lord!"

Strikingly it is not the sending alone that results in the salvation of the world. As observed above what matters to Paul is the whole scheme of the Christ-event. Indeed the sending resulted in one very specific occurrence that is the key to the meaning of the whole, that is:

The Death of Jesus Christ. More than any other part of the whole, indeed in relation to every part of the whole, Paul speaks of the death of Jesus, the cross of Christ, for in the mind of the apostle this is the heart of the Christ-event. Notice that even though Paul speaks of the cross of Christ, two elements, the cross and the resurrection, are joined inseparably. One without the other is meaningless and, when either element is forced, distortion results. Without the resurrection the cross is the tragic end of an apparently good man, a failure of human justice, the result of the worst sort of pragmatism. Yet without the cross the resurrection does not hold its Christian meaning, for the one who is raised remains the one who was crucified and it is this very one whom Christians confess to be Lord.

This message may be a Pauline emphasis, but it was not a Pauline invention. As for the sending of God's Son, so also for his death, Paul seems to have inherited traditional ideas from his environment and other early Christians, though he clearly put these to his own use. How does Paul speak of the death of Jesus?

(1) Paul thinks of the death of God's Son, Jesus, as *obedience*. The apostle takes this line prominently in two texts, Rom 5:19 and Phil 2:8. Scholars generally relate the idea of obedience in Paul to an emerging pattern of thought in Hellenistic Judaism and subsequent Christianity, the notion of *humiliation that leads to exaltation*. This pattern of thought is widely attested in sources like Isaiah, various pieces of Jewish apocalyptic literature, Philo, Corpus Hermeticum Tractate 1 (Poimandres), Wisdom, Acts of Thomas ("The Hymn of the Pearl"), and the Similitudes of Ethiopic Enoch. In these documents

a variety of model figures engage in the pattern of humiliation-exaltation: the Suffering Servant, the Son of Man, the Logos, Wisdom, the Anthropos, Second Adam, the Righteous One, and a gnostic primal Redeemer-Man.

In each of these documents the chief figure is humbled and then exalted. The various literature with the various figures has in common the conviction that the humiliation-exaltation is vicariously valuable for humans. Early Christians appear to have used this motif to express their own conviction of the salvific value of Jesus' death. But again Christian thinking is distinct from similar expressions in that the saving humiliation-exaltation is proclaimed in terms of a specific historical person, Jesus. Paul seems to put a peculiarly Pauline twist on this line of thought in that he does not merely announce humiliation earning exaltation by descent and ascent; indeed the saving provision for humanity is stamped with a cruciform character! Thus Paul does not dangle a possibility before humans and admonish them to take advantage of it; rather he declares that God established the salvation of humanity in the crucifixion-resurrection of Jesus.

(2) Paul also thinks of the death of Jesus in relation to *sacrifice*. True, Paul never calls the death a sacrifice per se, but he employs various sacrificial images from the Hebrew Bible for interpreting the significance of Jesus' death. First, the idea of an "expiatory sin offering" informs Paul's thought in several places. Specifically, at Rom 3:25 the word *mercy-seat* (Greek: *hilastērion*) bespeaks the notion that the death of Christ covered, or dealt with, the sin of humankind, and so Christ's death ended the bondage of humanity to sin. This idea is probably one important element behind Paul's statements that Christ died "for us" or "for our sin" or "for our sins" (1 Cor 11:24; Gal 1:4; Rom 4:25; 6:10). Second, Paul refers to Christ's death as the seal of the new covenant (1 Cor 11:25). The old covenant was that of the law with its promise of *forgiveness* upon the basis of repentance, but the new covenant is that of the *delivery* of humanity, by God acting to establish a new covenant through Christ's death, for freedom (Gal 1:4; 5:1). Third, Paul can use the idea of the Passover lamb to interpret the death of Jesus (it is not certain the Passover lamb was thought of as a sacrifice by Jews in the first century). 1 Cor 5:7 declares, "Christ our paschal lamb is slain!" Remember it was the marking out of Israel with the blood of the Passover lamb that made the passing

over of the death angel possible (see Ex 12) and which brought about the exodus of Israel from Egypt to Canaan. This notion is likely one element behind Paul's declaration that Christ delivered Christians from wrath (1 Thess 1:10) and the pitfalls of the present evil age (Gal 1:4). One sees here in a variety of ways the early Christian tendency to apply models from Jewish sacrifice to the death of Jesus for the purpose of explicating the salvific value of that death.

(3) Another way Paul speaks of the death of Christ is as *redemption*. Several texts express this idea, but 1 Cor 6:20a provides a clear example of this interpretation, saying, "For you were purchased at a price!" (see also Gal 3:13; 4:5; 1 Cor 7:23). The thinking here has its background in the Greco-Roman world where slaves were occasionally bought free, often in the name of a god. This image is applied to Jesus' death, though somewhat vaguely. What distinguishes this interpretation is that a notion, not necessarily religious, is taken as a metaphor for Christological exposition wherein the idea of the "price paid" is likened to Jesus' death. This metaphor communicates that Jesus' death produces liberation, but it is not clear *from what* those now redeemed were bought. Notice, however, that the price was paid *by God,* and the purpose of the redemption was to bring to realization the promises of God, namely, the gift of the Spirit (Gal 3:14).

In sum, all these images relating to the death of Jesus express the conviction that powerful consequences extend from the cross of Christ. Sin was defeated. The law now has no claim on humanity. Indeed humanity is reconciled to God and now lives in freedom from past enslavements.

Conclusions

Paul's good news is his proclamation about God's Son, Jesus the Christ. The apostle teaches that Christ's whole linearity is an act of God (2 Cor 5:19). God sent his Son for the benefit of humanity, and the outcome of that sending was the crucifixion and resurrection of the Son. Paul says this means that humans are delivered (1 Thess 1:10), reconciled (Rom 5:1–11, esp. v. 10), as God through Christ defeats the forces of sin (Rom 6:11). Thus humans are liberated for new life now (Gal 4:5; Rom 6:4, 11) that is lived for Christ (2 Cor

5:14–15; Rom 7:4) and, in turn, for a future share in the resurrection (1 Thess 4:14; Rom 6:5).

BIBLIOGRAPHY

J. A. Fitzmyer, "The Gospel in the Theology of Paul," *Int* 33 (1979) 339–50.

R. H. Fuller, "Jesus Christ as Savior in the New Testament," *Int* 35 (1981) 145–56.

M. Hengel, *The Atonement* (Philadelphia: Fortress, 1981).

Idem, The Son of God (Philadelphia: Fortress, 1976).

L. E. Keck, *Paul and His Letters* (Philadelphia: Fortress, 1979) esp. chapter 3.

B. Lindars, *New Testament Apologetic* (London: SCM, 1961).

C. F. D. Moule, *The Origin of Christology* (Cambridge: University Press, 1977).

J. A. Ziesler, *Pauline Christianity* (Oxford: University Press, 1983).

Paul on the Law

In considering "the world of Paul and his readers" we saw how the law functioned in the Judaism of Paul's day. It is not necessary to repeat that discussion; rather the focus here is on what Paul as a Christian apostle has to say about the law in the light of the Christ-event. As we have seen Paul understands the present to be the juncture of the ages, or as a time in which there is a mingling of the present evil age and the new creation (1 Cor 10:11; 2 Cor 5:16). This juncture came about in and through the cross of Christ (1 Cor 1:17–18), and one of the most significant results is that *the law has been exposed for what it is*.

Paul declares that the law has no bearing on the Christian. It came after the promise of God to Abraham, the fulfillment of which was none other than Christ himself (Gal 3:15–18; Rom 3:31–4:25). In fact, Paul says the law did not come from God but from the angels (Gal 3:19–20). This denial of the divine authorship of the law does not besmirch the law which is, in fact, holy, just, and good (Rom 7:11); it merely identifies the law as a piece of information about the will of God. As an accurate statement of the way that is acceptable to God, the law has no inherent capacity to provide strength to humanity for the faithful execution of the stated, divine will (Rom 3:31–4:25; 7:7–12).

Furthermore from other of Paul's comments on the law one learns there is a tragic dimension with regard to humanity's involvement with the law. Sin (which Paul understood to be an active force) used the law to deceive humanity. Indeed sin used the law to trick humans into thinking that they could keep the law and thereby ingratiate themselves to God. Thus the law became, under the manipulation of sin, a deadly illusion (Rom 7:7–12).

Nevertheless, God allowed the law to function, even under the influence of sin, as a warden for the constraint of humanity (Gal 3:24–25). Although it was in the hands of sin, God made positive use of the law by having it make humanity conscious of its failures, its sinfulness! But still humans fell victim to the deception that through the law they could participate in a system that made them righteous, and so God intervened in Christ in order to discharge humanity from the curse of the law (Gal 3:14–15; Rom 7:4–6).

Therefore what may one say about the law in Paul's writings?

The law constitutes something of an enigma. On the one hand, it is sin's tool, a deception, from which humanity needs to be set free. On the other hand, it is not against the promise(s) of God and, in fact, in faith the Christian fulfills the law (Gal 3:21; Rom 3:31)! The intention of the law, as information from angels for the benefit of humanity, is good (Rom 7:7–12). Nevertheless, used by sin, the law is a damning illusion (Rom 7:11). Yet even though the law, under the influence of sin, is a servant of evil, God allows it to serve a positive role (Gal 3:24–25; Rom 7).

The cross of Christ, however, has exposed the law. The law is not overthrown because it was never in a position to be overthrown (Gal 3:21–22; Rom 3:31). Rather from a Christian perspective Paul says the law is a valid statement of information about God's will—it is nothing more or less! Thus the law is powerless and always was, first, because it came after the promise (Gal 3:15–18; Rom 4) and, second, because of the foibles of the flesh (Gal 3:21; Rom 8:3). Thus, while the law has been a deception (Rom 7:7–20), it has no present validity (Gal 4:4–6; 5:1–12). Yet it continues to constitute a threat to the believer (Gal 1:6–7; 4:3–11; Rom 7:1–12). The law, however, belongs to the old age (Gal 3 and 4; 5:12) and has no place in the new creation (Gal 3:25–29; 4:8–11; Rom 7:1–6).

In sum, Paul's presentation of the law appears to be an enigma in his writings because he simultaneously views it as (1) good but inherently impotent and (2) a tool of sin. Yet one should recognize that this perspective on the law came about after (or when?) Paul encountered the risen Christ. Thus his statements are a Christian confession in hindsight. While he was a practicing Jew Paul was more than a little content with his involvement with the law. Only after God revealed Christ to him did Paul perceive what he later says about the law.

BIBLIOGRAPHY

J. C. Beker, "The Enigma of the Law: Instrument of God or Servant of Sin?" in his *Paul the Apostle* (2d ed.; Philadelphia: Fortress, 1984) 235–54.

J. A. Fitzmyer, "Paul and the Law" in his *To Advance the Gospel* (New York: Crossroad, 1981) 186–201.

R. Jewett, "The Law and the Coexistence of Jews and Gentiles in Romans," *Int* 39 (1985) 341–56.

E. P. Sanders, "Patterns of Religion in Paul and Rabbinic Judaism: A Holistic Method of Comparison," *HTR* 66 (1973) 455–78.

Idem, Paul, the Law, and the Jewish People (Philadelphia: Fortress, 1983).

H. J. Schoeps, "Paul's Misunderstanding of the Law" in W. A. Meeks, ed., *The Writings of St. Paul* (Norton Critical Edition: New York: Norton, 1972) 349–60.

And for those who read German, a response to Schoeps is F. Mussner's "Hat Paulus das Gesetz 'misverstanden'?" in his *Der Galaterbrief* (Freiburg: Herder, 1977) 188–204.

Eschatology

To begin this consideration of Paul's eschatology, it is necessary to make three interrelated observations. The first two are the results of the foregoing critical examination of the letters of the Pauline corpus and the third is a statement of fact. First, by understanding apocalyptic patterns as the framework of Paul's thought, one creates the need for an exact definition of *eschatology*, since the two are often taken synonymously. In this section "eschatology" literally means "teaching about the end." Second, the decisions made earlier in this study concerning authorship of the various letters result in the exclusion of six letters from this synthetic examination of eschatology. Therefore the extensive eschatological scheme laid out in 2 Thess 2:1–12 does not play a part in what follows. Third, Paul never describes the age to come. He does refer to "the day of the Lord," but nothing specific is said about what makes up or goes on in the age to come, that is, the new creation or the kingdom of God.

The Day of the Lord

Paul writes about "the day of the Lord," apparently meaning to designate the last day of the present evil age and the first day of the consummated kingdom (see 1 Thess 5:2; 1 Cor 1:8; 3:13; 5:5; 2 Cor 1:14). The apostle delineates certain events that will occur on that day. He tells his readers that Christ will come, descending from heaven. Thus this day is the one on which the crucified, risen, exalted Lord will return (see 1 Thess 4:13–18; 1 Cor 15:12–58; Phil 3:17–4:1). At Christ's return the dead "in Christ" will be raised; and as the dead in Christ are raised, so there is the synergistic gathering of the living with them (1 Thess 4:13–18; 1 Cor 15:20–28). Moreover at Christ's coming all will be changed, the living and the dead, as they put on an immortal resurrection body (1 Cor 15:35–58). Then occurs the destruction of every rule, authority, and power—notice Christ rules now as a result of the resurrection but he has not yet destroyed (though he has apparently defeated) his enemies (1 Cor 15:12–58, especially v. 25). With his victory completed Christ presents the kingdom to God, and then Christ is himself subjected to the Lordship of God (1 Cor 15:24–28). Paul declares that at this time every knee in heaven, on earth, and under the earth shall bow and every tongue confess that Jesus Christ is Lord to the glory of God the Father (Phil 2:9–11).

In brief Paul thinks of the day of the Lord as (1) the day of salvation (2 Cor 6:2) and (2) the day of wrath and fury (Rom 2:5–9). Both salvation and wrath are the results of God's judgment (Rom 2:16; also 2 Cor 5:10). Thus with an eye toward the day of the Lord Paul warns:

1. those doing the works of the flesh shall not inherit the kingdom of God (Gal 5:19–21);

2. the unrighteous will not inherit the kingdom of God (1 Cor 6:9–11);

3. the enemies of the cross of Christ have their end in destruction (Phil 3:17–21).

On the other hand Paul exhorts the Christians to live and walk in the Spirit, for those who are and that which is "in the Spirit" have their inheritance in the kingdom of God (Gal 5:22–26; 1 Cor 6:9–11).

The Kingdom of God

Paul alludes to the kingdom of God as the realm of God's *power* and *Spirit* (Gal 5:19–26; 1 Cor 4:20). He juxtaposes this realm to *unrighteousness* and the *flesh* (Gal 5:19–21; 1 Cor 6:9–11). But the apostle does not describe the kingdom in specific terms other than to tell the readers what the characteristics of the Spirit are, as fruit of the Spirit (see Gal 5:22–23).

A Summary Statement with Regard to Pauline Eschatology

Paul registers three main points as he offers eschatology to various early Christian communities. First, Christians living at the juncture of the ages await Christ's coming at the absolute end of the present evil age (Phil 3:17–4:1). Second, the time of Christ's coming is unknown, but it will occur suddenly (Paul probably thinks it will be soon—see 1 Thess 4:15); and therefore Christians should not only expect Christ but be prepared to meet him by being watchful (1 Thess 4.13–5:11). Third, because Christ is coming the Christians should *live in hope* and *encourage one another* (1 Thess 4:18; 5:11).

In addition to these major points, which should be readily apparent, the reader of Paul's letters can draw out other conclusions from the eschatological statements the apostle makes. One should recognize however that at times the ice becomes pretty thin in such a treatment.

One seemingly sure conclusion from Paul's eschatological statements is that Christians have assurance as "those washed, sanctified, and justified in the name of the Lord Jesus Christ and in the Spirit of God" of an inheritance in God's kingdom (1 Cor 6). But this leads to the question, "What about others, that is, non-Christians?" In offering an answer one finds the ice starts to grow thin.

Nevertheless, one can observe that Paul says:

1. the unrighteous will not inherit the kingdom of God (1 Cor 6);
2. the enemies of the cross end in destruction (Phil 3:19);
3. wrath and fury come on evil-doers (Rom 2:5–9).

For understanding these statements two other texts are helpful. (1) Gal 5:19–25 says those doing works of the flesh shall not inherit the kingdom. Notice, however, that this text does not say that those doing the works of the Spirit shall; rather those who live "in the Spirit" inherit the kingdom. (2) 1 Thess 2:16 says the wrath of God *is* upon disobedient Jews *until* the end (see above on 1 Thessalonians)—similarly see Rom 1:18–2:16.

Now what does all this mean? To anticipate, it appears that Paul thinks that in the end *all human beings (plus the created order?) will be saved.* Why? Paul says that as a result of the cross of Christ a division has been made between *that in the flesh* and *that in the Spirit*, or, in other words, between *that designated for wrath* and *that designated for salvation*. While the ultimate form of distinguishing between these categories takes place at the end (on the day of the Lord), already lines are drawn so that wrath is revealed and some are being saved. At the end the effect of God's dividing will be like a fire's burning (see 1 Cor 3:13–15), so that some things will be consumed and others will survive. Clearly that which is "in the flesh" is destined for destruction (see 2 Cor 5:10). The result of this fiery judgment is that God *purifies* and, thereby, saves humanity. Thus certain lines in Paul's letter become intelligible:

1 Cor 15:22 says *all* are made alive by Christ.

2 Cor 5:14 says Christ died for *all* and, therefore, *all* have died.

Rom 11:25–26 says the *fullness* of the Gentiles and *all* Israel will be saved.

Rom 11:32 says God consigned *all* to disobedience in order that he may have mercy upon *all*.

Phil 2:9–11 says "in the name of Christ" *every* knee will bow and *every* tongue will confess that Jesus Christ is Lord.

Phil 3:17–21 says the Christians await a Savior, the Lord Jesus Christ, who "will transform our humble bodies to like form with his glorious body by means of the power that enables him even to subjugate all things to himself."

It seems that Paul is persuaded that ultimately *all* will be saved by the power of God in Christ, though not under the same conditions. Those whose lives and labors have essentially been devoted to works of the flesh will suffer the loss of their worthless efforts (see 1 Cor 3:12–15). But those whose lives have been lived "in the Lord" shall find their labors were not in vain (see 1 Cor 15:58). Indeed the labors of those who lived and worked in the Lord will survive God's fiery testing and their refined efforts will be their reward!

As a possibility one should admit that there may be those whose lives and labors are so thoroughly useless that, once tested, nothing will remain. This possibility, however, is not a subject Paul addresses. (C. S. Lewis offers a creative treatment of the subject in his book, *The Great Divorce*.) The fact is that in his eschatological teaching Paul does not focus in a major way on the down side of God's power that is wrath; instead he labors to proclaim the up side that is the awesome love of God expressed and at work in Jesus Christ.

The Spirit

Given the situational nature of Paul's writings it should go without saying that Paul does not offer a doctrine of the spirit, a *pneumatology*. Rather in the course of his writings Paul often speaks about "spirit"— indeed, one hundred and twenty times! There is, however, a somewhat confusing diversity in Paul's use of the word *spirit* (Greek: *pneuma*). The apostle uses *spirit* so as to indicate three distinct *spirits:* the anthropological, the demonological, and the theological. For the purposes of this study we shall lay aside the unquestionably anthropological and demonological uses in order to focus on the theological spirit-statements. In other words, the concern here is to understand what Paul thought about the Holy Spirit. In pursuit of this goal this section does not study possible backgrounds from which Paul may have drawn inspiration for his thinking about the spirit. Instead it surveys the pattern of Paul's usage of *pneuma* to see *what Paul said about the spirit*.

Paul on the Holy Spirit

Examination of the theological spirit-statements in Paul's letters finds that the statements are not all of one cloth. Sometimes the apostle speaks simply about "the spirit," but at other times he speaks of "the holy spirit," "the spirit of God," or "the spirit of Christ."

Essentially the idea behind all these phrases is that of *the power and presence of God*. Inherently, in terms of language and thought, this notion is not a unique concept; for Paul shares the basic idea of "the spirit" as the presence and power of God with both Jewish and non-Jewish writers of his day. But Paul gives this concept of the spirit a distinctively Christian cast when and as he relates it to Jesus Christ, especially to his death and resurrection. 1 Cor 15:45 is a good illustration of the Christian twist on Paul's thinking about the spirit; there Paul says, "Thus it is written, 'The first man Adam became a living being'; the last Adam became a life-giving spirit."

But despite this distinctly Christian understanding of the spirit, Paul's pneumatological thought remains something of an enigma. It is possible, however, to achieve further clarity on what Paul thought about the spirit by studying his writings, for while the apostle does not stop in his letters and offer a systematic doctrine of the spirit, he does make a number of statements that reveal more specific information about his understanding of the presence and power of God. Briefly sketched, these remarks tell one the following about Paul's thinking about the spirit:

1. The spirit is, on the one hand, God's life-giving power; and, on the other hand, it is a gift received by humanity (Gal 3:2; 2 Cor 1:22; Rom 15:13, 16).
2. The spirit marks a realm (Gal 5:16, 19, 25; 1 Cor 6:11).
3. The spirit is an avenue for and an agent of God's revelation (1 Cor 2:13; 12:3; 2 Cor 3:17).
4. The spirit sustains the Christians, that is, those "in" the realm of the spirit (Rom 8:9–11).
5. As one is "in the spirit" or as the spirit dwells in one (Rom 8:11), one is sanctified by the spirit (Rom 15:16).
6. The spirit is the second part of God's salvific sending. First, God sent the Son to redeem those under the law so that they might be adopted; then, because they are adopted, God sent or sends the spirit (here, of his Son) crying, "Abba! Father!" (Gal 4:4–6).
7. The spirit intercedes for those "in the spirit" and "in whom" the spirit dwells, thereby helping humans in their weakness (Rom 8:26). This activity of the spirit indicates that humans are children of God as the spirit (here, of God) moves the human spirit to cry, "Abba! Father!" (Rom 8:14–16).
8. The spirit bears fruit in the life of the Christians, specifically as listed in Gal 5:22–23.
9. The spirit enables the gifts manifested in the lives of the Christians (1 Cor 12).

10. The spirit is the hallmark of the new creation, being given to all Christians (1 Cor 12 and 14); thus, the spirit is not a private matter.

The Spirit as a Sign

Paul's writings reveal that he understands the spirit to be something less than the end-all and be-all of the riches of Christ. Indeed, Paul thinks the spirit is but a token of the full riches of God; and so Paul refers to the spirit as a promise (Gal 3:14), the first-fruit (Rom 8:23), and a guaranteeing payment (Greek: *arrabōn*; 2 Cor 1:22).

But what is it that the spirit is a sign of? Apparently it is the power and presence of God in the time between the cross-resurrection of Jesus and the coming of the risen exalted Lord in glory. Thus *the spirit is the sign of the full form of reconciliation that will be achieved on the day of the Lord.* Paul can say there are many gifts of the spirit, but there is only one spirit in whom all those manifesting gifts of the spirit are held together (1 Cor 12:4). The spirit is, therefore, the sign of the Christians' reconciliation to God; it is their bond to God (1 Cor 6:17). Moreover it is a sign of the reconciliation of the various factions of humanity to one another; it yields their common good (1 Cor 12:7).

Conclusions

Paul understands the spirit to be the power of God at work in the present in defiance of the power of sin. In short, the spirit is the power of God grasping Christians and saving them at the juncture of the ages. The spirit liberates Christians and sustains them in their God-achieved freedom, enabling insight and a new relation to God. Yet there is no suggestion by Paul that this power makes the present day Christians into totally new creatures. Rather the spirit is a promise of the full, future transformation, and currently it identifies Christians with Christ. (It is striking how thoroughly this understanding fits the apocalyptic scheme that underlies Paul's general thought about the saving work of God in Christ.)

BIBLIOGRAPHY

J. A. Fitzmyer, "The Lord and the Spirit" in *Pauline Theology* (Englewood Cliffs: Prentice-Hall, 1967) 41–43.

R. Jewett, "Spirit," *IDBSup* 839–41.

G. W. H. Lampe, "Holy Spirit," *IDB* 2.626–39.

S. V. McCasland, "Spirit," *IDB* 4.432–34.

P. W. Meyer, "The Holy Spirit in the Pauline Letters: A Contextual Exploration," *Int* 32 (1979) 3–18.

E. Schweizer, *The Holy Spirit* (Philadelphia: Fortress, 1980).

Anthropological Terms

What was Paul's view of humanity? Scholars argue whether Paul had this or that view of the human condition, and the debate is often lively; for many interpreters, though they articulate radically different explanations of Paul's anthropology, maintain that the apostle's understanding of humanity is the key to the whole of his theology. A fundamental ingredient in such debates is the words Paul uses in reference to humans. These include "the inner/outer person" (Greek: *esō/ exō anthrōpos*), "heart" (Greek: *kardia*), "mind" (Greek: *nous*), "spirit of humanity" (Greek: *pneuma tou anthrōpou*), "flesh" (Greek: *sarx*), "body" (Greek: *sōma*), "conscience" (Greek: *syneidēsis*), and "soul" or "life" (Greek: *psychē*).

There was a time, not long ago, when it was easy to draw lines between interpreters of Paul on the subject of the apostle's anthropology. Such division was possible because scholars tended to gravitate toward either Jewish or Hellenistic (non-Jewish) backgrounds as the key to Paul's anthropological thought. This approach, still detectable in some studies of Paul's writings and theology, operates in the following manner. First, the interpreter determines that a particular background is the correct one against which to view Paul's statements about humanity. Second, all occurrences of a particular term or terms are noted. Third, the various uses of the term(s) are classified as technical, casual, traditional, or even atypical—depending on how they relate to the declared definitive background. Fourth, the meaning of the term is explicated in relation to the framework of the definitive background.

All such studies may be criticized for taking words out of their natural linguistic contexts and fitting them into a putatively meaningful framework that was provided by the interpreter. The result of these interpretative exercises is that language is abstracted and, thereby, so is Pauline anthropology. Moreover questionable backgrounds and putative lines of influence are allowed to control interpretation.

The results of such forced readings of Paul are almost comical. One interpreter suggests Paul's writings show changing meaning for words so that one sees in Paul's letters that the definition of certain words changed. Another critic posits a process of evolution from Jewish to Hellenistic terminology. Perhaps the most famous and influential example is R. Bultmann's contention that Paul's primitive language is expressive of a way of understanding humanity that is practically identical to twentieth century Existentialism. Bultmann rigorously abstracts Paul's anthropological terms and imbues them with existentialist meaning; but even in his rigor Bultmann finds it necessary to distinguish between Paul's *significant* (those uses that could be fitted to Existentialism) and *casual* (those uses that did not fit Existentialism) employment of terms. Predictably, Bultmann claims that only *significant* uses really express Paul's anthropology. So convincing is Bultmann's description of Pauline anthropology along the lines of Existentialism that his student G. Bornkamm can easily and conveniently name and define Paul's anthropological terms in the space of four and a half pages of his book on Paul.

Nevertheless, things are not so clear as some interpreters might have one think. The difficulty in grasping what Paul thinks about humanity is not only that he uses a variety of terms or that he never stops and says, "Here's what I think about the human condition," but also that the apostle uses each of the various terms relating to humanity in a variety of ways. For example, *body* is used throughout Paul's letters in a non-technical fashion to indicate *the observable, material human self.* But at certain points in the letters *sōma* takes on a technical sense as *the basis of human relationship* (see 1 Cor 6; 10; 11); furthermore, in reference to the life of the church, *body* becomes a metaphor, "the body of Christ," to explain the necessary interrelatedness of the diverse Christian "gifts." (We will return to this point in the section on "ecclesiology.") In a similar manner one observes that *flesh* takes on a variety of meanings as Paul uses it in different contexts. At 1 Cor 15:39–40 *sarx* seems completely interchangeable with *sōma*, indicating *the observable self.* Then, at Phil 1:22 the word has the apparently neutral sense of *present bodily existence.* Yet, in

3:4; Gal 3:3; 4:23; and 5:16–21, *flesh* indicates a demonic sphere of power juxtaposed to *spirit*. (We will return to this later.)

Furthermore, not only do terms carry various meanings, but the framework of Paul's anthropology vacillates. Sometimes Paul thinks and expresses himself in terms of a dichotomous Jewish anthropology of body and spirit/soul (see 1 Cor 7:34; 2 Cor 7:1), and at other times he employs a Hellenistic trichotomy of body, soul, and spirit (see 1 Thess 5:23). The reason for this diversity in anthropological terminology and even in the framework for thinking and speaking about humanity is that *for Paul anthropology is derived from theology.* Paul uses a variety of anthropological terms and different points of view (frameworks) with striking flexibility in relation to theological controversies he faced. In other words, the center of Paul's thought is not anthropological; rather at the heart of the apostle's thinking is an apocalyptic concept of God and God's saving action in Christ, summed up in the phrase "the righteousness of God." While this central theological conviction provides the anchor for the apostle's thinking and teaching, he employs one anthropological term or perspective here and another there to score the theological point he desires to make. To borrow language recently made well-known by J. C. Beker, anthropology is part of the contingency of Paul's thought, not part of its coherent center. In Paul's mind humanity is part of God's creation. Humans are creatures who, along with the cosmos, are being saved. Indeed God's cosmic work of redemption is seen in microcosm as the human or humanity is saved. Thus Paul's comments about humanity are determined by the points the apostle strives to make about God.

A final illustration demonstrates and clarifies this understanding of Paul's anthropology. Let us again consider *flesh.* We saw that this word is used variously to indicate the observable self, human existence, and a sphere of power opposite of spirit. How can the apostle move from the literal to the metaphorical (some would say the esoteric!)? Strikingly, there is logic in Paul's use of *sarx.* Because the flesh is what is circumcised, the word is capable of symbolizing the realm of human, systemic righteousness, a realm coupled with the power of sin in the mind of the apostle. Thus *flesh* is not a power but it indicates a realm in which the power of sin operates. As L. E. Keck observes, "Because Spirit is the power-sphere of the new age, flesh is the power-sphere of the old age." The difference is that the spirit is the power-sphere of the old age." The difference is that the spirit is both realm and power whereas the flesh is merely realm. Thus humans are, on the one hand, *flesh*—a neutral fact; but, on the other hand, without God's gracious presence and power, they are *in the flesh*—a tragic fact! Yet, delivered from sin by God's work in Christ, humans are no longer in the flesh; they are *in the spirit,* transformed in the realm of God's new creation.

BIBLIOGRAPHY

Generally see the various articles on relevant anthropological terms in *IDBSup.*

J. C. Beker, *Paul the Apostle* (2d ed; Philadelphia: Fortress, 1984).

G. Bornkamm, *Paul* (New York: Harper & Row, 1971).

R. Bultmann, *The Theology of the New Testament,* 2 vols. (New York: Scribner's Sons, 1951/1955).

R. Jewett, *Paul's Anthropological Terms: A Study of Their Use in Conflict Settings* (AGJU 10; Leiden: Brill, 1971).

E. Käsemann, "On Paul's Anthropology" in his *Perspectives on Paul* (Philadelphia: 1971).

L. E. Keck, *Paul and His Letters* (Philadelphia: Fortress, 1979).

J. Murphy-O'Connor, *Becoming Human Together: The Pastoral Anthropology of St. Paul* (Good News Studies 2; Wilmington: Glazier, 1982).

D. E. H. Whiteley, *The Theology of St. Paul* (Oxford: Blackwell, 1964).

Ecclesiology

The only appropriate starting point for a discussion of Pauline *ecclesiology* is with the candid admission that Paul offered no "doctrine of the church." He did, however, use the word *church* frequently; and he wrote enough about the church in his letters that one may infer something of what he thought about it. Yet, to discuss Pauline ecclesiology is to create an abstraction that Paul himself never created; and so, one must proceed with extreme caution.

A Starting Point

One way to begin a consideration of Paul's thinking about the church is to ask, "Why is there a church?" According to Paul the church exists because of the activity of God in Jesus Christ. In his earliest letter, 1 Thessalonians, Paul writes to "the church of the Thessalonians" (1:1), and as 1 Thess 1:10 indicates, this church exists because Jesus delivered certain people from the wrath to come. As we have seen in considering Paul's thinking about the Spirit, those whom God-in-Christ delivered are now in a new realm; namely, they are "in the Spirit."

Paul addressed those in this new realm to whom he writes as "the church." The Greek word Paul used is *ekklēsia*. This is the word the translators of the Septuagint chose to render the Hebrew word *qāhāl*, which designated the assembly of the Israelites both in their desert wanderings (Deut 23:2) and in their later liturgical gatherings (1 Kgs 8:55). (*Qāhāl* is sometimes still used to name various synagogues of contemporary Jews.) Another word, perhaps freer from traditional theological associations, that may be used to translate *ekklēsia* is *congregation*.

The word *church* or *congregation* as a designation for those in the new realm implies that Christianity is no private matter. Rather, to be a Christian is to be a member of a congregation wherein there is the mutual experience of God's grace. The new life that those in the new realm live is lived together as a God-created experience of unity.

As with most words that Paul used, *church* has more shades than one. Indeed, *ekklēsia* has two clear uses in Paul's writings. On the one hand, the dominant meaning of *church* designates a local church—as in 1 Thess 1:1; 1 Cor 1:2; Phlm 2. On the other hand, Paul can speak of "the church" in such a manner that he must mean to indicate the whole Christian community in the world—as in 1 Cor 10:32; 12:28; Phil 3:6. Thus, in terms of its nature, Paul seems to think of "the church" primarily in terms of local congregations; but these geographically distinguishable churches do not exist in isolation from one another any more than does a Christian experience the presence and power of God in remove from others who are in the realm of the Spirit. This observation brings us conveniently and naturally to what many scholars regard as Paul's own distinctive contribution to thinking about the church.

Body of Christ

In considering Paul's letters to the church in Corinth, especially 1 Corinthians, we saw that a serious problem existed in the Corinthian church that threatened the unity of that congregation. Some of the Corinthians were focusing on the idea of *spirit* and *spiritual things* to the point that factions had cropped up and individual spiritual superiority was being paraded in diverse ways. Paul perceived that this arrogant, individualistic preoccupation with spirituality had the potential to destroy the Corinthian congregation by exploding it into manifold cliques and pious personalities. Therefore, Paul wrote to correct the problem.

To those in orbit over *the spirit* Paul offered a concrete comedown: he talked about *the body*. Indeed, he used the word (*sōma*) forty-three times in writing 1 Corinthians, about twice as many uses as in all his other letters combined! At its basic level of meaning in Paul's use *body* was the observable, material human self, i.e., the exact antithesis of the quasi-gnostic notion of *spirit* over which the Corinthian congregation was splitting apart. But as we saw in considering Paul's anthropological terms, *body* can and does also indicate that which is the basis of relationships. In correcting the Corinthians, Paul appears to have grasped this second dimension of *body* and gone so far in his meditation that he employed the word ultimately as a metaphor for what it meant for the Corinthians to be a *church*. 1 Cor 12:12–26 develops this metaphor to the point that in 1 Cor 12:27 Paul can say to the Corinthians, "You are the body of Christ." Notice that Paul did not say outright that the church is the body of Christ; that development came into Christian thinking about the church in the writing of the author of Colossians and was developed to its loftiest height in Ephesians.

Further Consideration of "Body of Christ" and Pauline Ecclesiology

At first glance this line of development in Paul's thinking might strike one as odd, but it certainly would not have seemed so to Paul's readers in Corinth. In fact, popular Stoic philosophy knew and used the metaphor of a body with different parts in order to describe a community. Many scholars see in 1 Cor 12:14–27 an undeniable reflection of this then-common Stoic metaphor. Whether, in fact, this is correct is irrelevant. The main lessons to be gathered from such a parallel are that Paul resorted to neither the esoteric nor the unreasonable in addressing his readers and in reflecting upon what it meant for those delivered by the power of God to live as a/the church; moreover, his readers would have been able quite easily to get his point.

As Paul did not articulate an ecclesiology, so he did not delineate a church order, polity, or organization. For Paul the church, even in its universal dimension, was not an institution but a collection of redeemed sinners, called saints, and bound together as mutual recipients of the powerful grace of God. According to Paul the discernible evidence of God's grace was the manifestation of the different gifts of the Spirit as different, but complementary, functions in the church. The purpose of these gifts was not to provide a means for ranking or comparing one Christian to another; rather, the gifts were given in their different forms for the upbuilding of the church—local and universal. One cannot read Paul's letters without perceiving his blazing concern for the edification of the church. This theme is found overtly and implicitly in and through every one of Paul's communications. And yet, he never set out a pattern for the church or lists ecclesiastical offices. For him, the structure and the leadership of the church(es) were dynamic, charismatic.

Finally, one must observe that ecclesiology never moves into the foreground in Paul's writing for all the reasons given—and, yet, for one other. In Paul's thought and writings the foremost position is always occupied by Christ and him crucified, the righteousness of God. But, as we have seen, a careful reader can discern some of Paul's thinking about the church from his letters—enough, in fact, for valuable insights to be gained.

BIBLIOGRAPHY

J. C. Beker, "The Church as the Dawning of the New Age" in his *Paul the Apostle* (2d ed.; Philadelphia: Fortress, 1984) 303–27.

E. Käsemann, "The Theological Problem Presented by the Motif of the Body of Christ" in his *Perspectives on Paul* (Philadelphia: Fortress, 1971) 102–21.

P. S. Minear, *Images of the Church in the New Testament* (Philadelphia: Westminster, 1960).

J. A. Ziesler, *Pauline Christianity* (Oxford: University Press, 1983).

Pauline Halakah:
The Ethical Teachings of Paul

Present day readers of Paul's letters usually react strongly to his writings, either by being attracted to Paul or by being turned off by him. Often, these reactions are to the practical dimension of his letters, since many people are neutral toward Paul's theology. They feel he had the right to think in his own way about God, the universe, and even humanity at the theological level. But these same people will be either fervent supporters or strident opponents of Paul's statements concerning everyday life, the church, and social order. It is, however, a mistake to view Paul's ethics in detachment from his theology, for it is precisely the apostle's thinking about God that led him to have whatever ethics he expresses.

Paul's Ethical Perspective

In order to understand Paul's ethical teachings it is necessary to see this dimension of his thought within the larger context of his theological vision. Time and again we have seen that Paul thought in relation to two cosmic realms that had been marked out, indeed created by God's powerful activity in Christ. Peculiar to Paul's thinking is the idea that he and those delivered into the realm of the Spirit live in a time when, with the death and resurrection of Jesus Christ, the new age has *already* begun; but, currently, the old era is passing away and the new aeon is *not yet* fully present. The new age will arrive in fullness at the *parousia* (the so-called "second coming") of Jesus Christ. Thus Paul's ethics were influenced by his anticipation of the

new era which he believed is *about to come*; or, in other words, he
expected an imminent parousia.

Another determinative factor in Paul's ethical thinking is his self-
image. He saw himself as an evangelist-pastor. He was constantly and
consistently oriented toward and motivated by his concern to build up
the Christian community. Therefore, his directives were not of a general sort, aimed at regulating the activity or lifestyles of those outside
the church; his only real concern for the non-Christian was that he or
she become a Christian. Indeed, Paul's thinking was so related to the
edification of the church that he did *not* direct the members of those
congregations to which he writes to engage in community service or
social action. While, as will be seen, Paul's ethical teaching opens
the door for present day Christian involvement in society, he never
walked through that door himself. As L. E. Keck says, "It would have
been ludicrous if he had urged small house churches to pretend that
they had civic responsibility."

To summarize, one sees three factors in Paul's thought that in-
fuenced his ethical pronouncements. First, he was not a casual letter
writer nor was he a systematic theologian. He wrote to congregations,
addressing specific problems that arose in the daily lives of the particular churches. He wrote as a pastor, and his letters are pastoral
throughout; they are written examples of Paul's constant concern to
build up the early Christian community. Second, one must recognize
that Paul's perspective was short-sighted. He believed he was living
at the turn of the ages and he lived expecting the coming of Christ
from heaven. He was confident that at Christ's coming the old order
would pass away fully and everything would be new, created afresh
by God; and so, he cared and spoke little about the structures of this
world—after all, they were condemned to pass away. Third, Paul and
the members of the first century church were in no position to dictate
policy to the powers in the world around them. Thriving churches did
exist in the capital cities of many provinces and of the empire; but
those early Christians were not, for the most part, people of elite social
status (although they were not, as many claim, the dregs of humanity).
They were slaves, former slaves, small-time merchants, and some few
from the noble classes—not so many in number, however, as to command a serious public hearing.

Contrasting Attitudes Toward Paul's Halakah

It is illuminating to compare ancient and modern attitudes toward Paul's ethics. In his own day, the apostle was perceived to be a dangerously liberal non-traditionalist. There seems to be understandable cause for this perception. At Gal 5:1, Paul states the bottom line of his ethics to a congregation that sought a system (the law) for right living: "For freedom Christ set us free; stand firm then and do not be bound in a yoke of slavery." At least one congregation took Paul's proclamation of freedom to an extreme that matched his fervent presentation. Members of the congregation in Corinth understood the freedom in Christ to mean that all things were lawful to them! (See Paul's quotation of the Corinthians' slogan in 1 Cor 6:13, "All things are lawful for me.") Paul tried to correct this misunderstanding of what he had said (he continues in 1 Cor 6:13, "But not all things are profitable . . . I will not be mastered by anything"), but the problem persisted as is evident in the ensuing controversy in Corinth attested in 2 Corinthians. Moreover, the word about Paul seems to have gotten around; for in writing to the church in Rome Paul had to labor to dispel a false perception of his message (see esp. Rom 6:1). It was his reputation as an iconoclast that caused his arrest in Jerusalem which ultimately brought his execution. Indeed, it is Paul's proclamation of "freedom" in Christ and his admonition to "walk in the Spirit" rather than to live by keeping certain rules that suggests the title of this section on Paul's theology: Pauline halakah. *Halakah* is a technical term in rabbinic writings for the directives for living that derive from the law itself. Paul states no formal system of "ethics"; he offers directions (pointers!) to Christians in particular situations, and these instructions are determined from his central vision of God's apocalyptic activity of reconciliation. Sometimes these directions were in the form of catalogues of virtues and vices that should or should not characterize Christian living. These are remarkably similar to lists in popular Stoic philosophy that described preferred contemporary social order, and Paul seems content to apply these descriptions to the Christian community. Yet, he was still perceived as a threat by many of his fellow Christians.

How strange it is that this man, once labeled a dangerous liberal, is today most often thought to be conservative, *too* conservative. For example, many present day readers find Paul's statements in 1 Cor 7 objectionable. He speaks there in relation to three phenomena: circumcision, slavery, and marriage. In the cases of circumcision and slavery Paul issues the imperative, "Stay put!" In regard to marriage he states his preference, "It is better to stay unmarried."

From the factors observed above as determinative for Paul's thought, one should understand that Paul *relativized* circumcision, slavery, and marriage. They count for nothing. Yet, modern Christians and non-Christians fault Paul for not declaring the injustice of slavery and for a seemingly negative attitude toward matrimony. Consider slavery, however, from Paul's own perspective: neither slavery nor freedom mattered, for the Christian slave was the Lord's free person and the free person was the Lord's slave. A primary concern with changing one's social status made the status more important than it should have been for one whose true status was determined in relation to God. What mattered for Paul was freedom in Christ. The reason worldly affairs did not matter was not that Paul was indifferent to reality, but rather that Paul believed he lived in the last hour and the form of this world was passing away. Thus, for Paul, striving for involvement with or change of the structures of this world was a waste of time and effort, for this world had no future.

Final Observations

In the last analysis what makes Paul appear conservative to a person living in the twentieth century is the loss of Paul's apocalyptic perspective. It is unfair to read Paul from the distance of 1,900 years in an era when people do not necessarily share his blazing persuasion that Jesus is coming soon. To read Paul fairly today, one must be sensitive to his horizon and seek to understand Paul's thinking in relation to the current situation.

When Paul argued that the Christian was not to be concerned to change his or her earthly status, he declared that the status quo was doomed to pass away. Paul saw God's sanction, not upon this present evil age, but upon the age of freedom in Jesus Christ which was "already but not yet." By depriving the present earthly structures of a divine sanction he opened the way for later Christians (who do not share exactly his view of an imminent parousia) to make necessary social changes. Paul clearly declared the earthly structures not to be in accordance with the will of God, and so the Christian living in this present age is freed by God's grace and in a new situation in relation to the Lord Jesus Christ.

Paul's ethics are not inherently *conservative* at all, for nothing of this age will be conserved or preserved. Paul said that the age to come will be a new creation. Thus he laid the foundation for Christian involvement in social change: If the institutions and powers of our world do not hold a divine sanction, indeed, if they are condemned by God to pass away, then they are open to change. To stand 1900 + years after Paul and continue to reiterate his words as a defense for social lethargy (using "justified by faith" to justify inertia with regard to the unjust structures of society) is to fail to realize the vision Paul had and for which he labored. If a reader of Paul wishes to find in his writing a motto for contemporary ethics, no passage is more appropriate than 1 Cor 3:10–15—Paul's undeniable admonition to do something in this world, by the grace of God, that will be worthy of the age to come!

BIBLIOGRAPHY

V. P. Furnish, *The Moral Teaching of Paul* (Nashville: Abingdon, 1973).

L. E. Keck, *Paul and His Letters* (Philadelphia: Fortress, 1979).

J. T. Sanders, *Ethics in the New Testament* (Philadelphia: Fortress, 1975).

Afterword

This book has been an effort to assist students of Paul in thinking about the apostle to the Gentiles, his life, his letters, and his theology. Most readers will have found that the book confronts them with a Paul whom they did not know before. I hope the encounter was gratifying in a number of ways. Paul as understood and presented here should unsettle many conventional assumptions and attitudes. I also hope that the encounter with a "new" Paul stimulated positive growth through reconsideration and reflection and that it did not create sheer distress because the reader perceived this work to be a threatening, non-traditional rereading of portions of the New Testament.

Moreover the apocalyptic key that this study applied to the Pauline lock may have struck the reader as an oddity. But I hope the reader did not take this theological framework to be a curious archaism. In coming to see that Paul perceived himself and all others to live at a time between the cross-resurrection and the coming of Christ, that is, at the juncture of the ages, one may have been able to appreciate and even appropriate the apostle's apocalyptic conviction into one's own theologizing. That the parousia (the coming of Christ in power and glory on the day of the Lord) did not happen in Paul's own time or in the ensuing 1900 + years in no way invalidates Paul's apocalyptic vision. It simply means that the juncture of the ends of the ages is a larger moment of time than the apostle understood it to be.

After reading this book and working through Paul's letters some may still dislike the Paul they come to know. I hope that is not the case, for this book rests on the conviction that increased understanding leads to increased sympathy, or at least increased tolerance. But the real purpose for the writing of this book will be fulfilled if someone is able to say, "I didn't understand Paul before. Now that I do, I find him and his vision of God truly compelling."

Appendix: Pauline Pseudepigrapha and Pseudepigraphy

The literature left by early Christians for their heirs (and later students) is not exhausted by the deposit of works comprising the canonical New Testament. Many works of the same genres as those of the New Testament (gospels, acts, epistles, and apocalypses) exist. A great number of these non-canonical works claim prominent New Testament figures as their authors. Paul is one of the early Christian leaders frequently named as author of non-canonical epistles.

Two prominent examples of such non-canonical Pauline letters are called *Laodiceans* and *3 Corinthians*. Because of matters of language (vocabulary, style, syntax), theology, the historical situations presupposed by the document, and the literary relation of these documents to canonical works (Laodiceans to Colossians and 3 Corinthians to 1 and 2 Corinthians) scholars universally judge that Laodiceans and 3 Corinthians do not come from Paul. This judgment has been shared by students of the Pauline literature through the centuries. Scholars suggest that some early Christians, wishing to honor Paul and/or preserve his apostolic teaching and/or appeal to his authority, wrote these letters in his name. Clearly the idea for the production of these letters comes from the references in the canonical letters to "lost" letters from Paul—Col 4:15–16 refers to a letter to the Laodiceans and 1 Cor 5:9; 2 Cor 2:3–4, 9; 7:8–12 refer to other letters from Paul to Corinth.

Laodiceans is a sheer pastiche of lines from other Pauline letters. The author offers nothing really original but lifts lines—primarily from Philippians, but also from 1 Thessalonians, Galatians, 1 Corinthians

(?), and Colossians—and assembles them into a *new* letter. 3 Corinthians is more original. It contains both lines from the canonical letters (Romans, 1 Corinthians, 2 Corinthians, Galatians, Ephesians, Philippians, 2 Thessalonians (?), 1 Timothy, and Philemon—also Luke and Acts) and somewhat elaborate traditional and confessional material not found elsewhere in Paul. Generally 3 Corinthians argues against heresy and shows a concern with a controversy over the resurrection.

If one agrees with the conclusion that these and other similar "Pauline" letters were not written by the apostle, then one should see that early Christians produced pseudonymous literature in Paul's name. Thus there is no question that, among the documents preserved from early Christianity, pseudepigraphical Pauline letters exist. The question, therefore, is not whether there are examples of pseudepigraphical Pauline letters. Clearly there are. The question becomes, "Are there instances of pseudepigraphical Pauline letters among those documents attributed to Paul in the New Testament?" This study holds that the six disputed letters (2 Thessalonians, Colossians, Ephesians, 1 Timothy, 2 Timothy, and Titus) attributed to Paul are themselves pseudepigraphical works.

BIBLIOGRAPHY

These texts are available in English with introductory discussions and annotations in

E. Hennecke, W. Schneemelcher, R. McL. Wilson, eds., *New Testament Apocrypha,* 2 vols. (Philadelphia: Westminster, 1963/1965—German originals 1959/1964).

Index of Authors

Index of Subjects

Index of Pauline Texts

Index of Other Ancient Texts

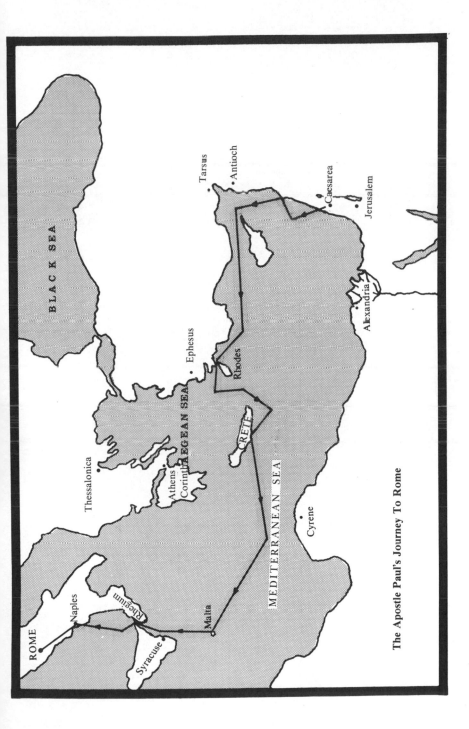

The Apostle Paul's Journey To Rome